Professional Collaboration With Purpose

Building on both cutting-edge research and professional learning practice, Amanda Datnow and Vicki Park explore how professional collaboration can support deeper learning for students and teachers alike. Although many schools and systems support teacher collaboration, they often fall short of their intended goals of improving teaching and learning. This book provides concrete guidance for creating the conditions for collaboration in which teachers are moved toward—rather than repelled by—joint work. The authors explore how collaborative settings can provide a space for working through the inevitable challenges that accompany the changing nature of teaching in the age of accountability and show the motivation, inspiration, and energy that teachers personally—and collectively—gain from collaborating to improve student learning. Ultimately, they show how teacher empowerment toward working together builds equitable and excellent learning environments.

Amanda Datnow is Professor in the Department of Education Studies and Associate Dean of Social Sciences at the University of California, San Diego.

Vicki Park is Assistant Professor of Educational Leadership at San Diego State University.

Routledge Leading Change Series
Series Editors:
Andy Hargreaves, *Boston College, USA*
Pak Tee Ng, *National Institute of Education, Nanyang Technological University, Singapore*

The world is crying out loud for quality education, and for the type of leadership and change to make quality education a reality. Never has there been a greater need for grasping the big pictures of leadership and change in education, which creates the world of tomorrow by developing future generations today.

In this series, you will find some of the world's leading intellectual authorities on educational leadership and change. From the pens of writers such as Dennis Shirley, Pak Tee Ng, Andy Hargreaves, Michael Fullan, Pasi Sahlberg, Alma Harris, Yong Zhao and Karen Edge, come wise insights and breakthrough ideas on this subject. They ask what the new imperatives of educational change are. They explore the paradoxical nature of educational change in celebrated Asian cultures and systems like those of Singapore. They point to the power of leading from the middle in schools, networks of schools and across the world, rather than just driving change from the top. They highlight the surreal nature of leadership and change at this critical moment in world history.

This series of books is for the stout-hearted reader who is keenly looking for inspiration to unlock the potential of educational leadership and change in this turbulent world.

The New Imperatives of Educational Change: Achievement with Integrity
Dennis Shirley

Learning from Singapore: The Power of Paradoxes
Pak Tee Ng

Surreal Change: The Real Life of Transforming Public Education
Michael Fullan

Professional Collaboration with Purpose: Teacher Learning Towards Equitable and Excellent Schools
Amanda Datnow and Vicki Park

For more information about this series, please visit: www.routledge.com/Routledge-Leading-Change-Series/book-series/RLCS

Professional Collaboration With Purpose
Teacher Learning Towards Equitable and Excellent Schools

Amanda Datnow and Vicki Park

NEW YORK AND LONDON

First published 2019
by Routledge
52 Vanderbilt Avenue, New York, NY 10017

and by Routledge
2 Park Square, Milton Park, Abingdon, Oxon, OX14 4RN

Routledge is an imprint of the Taylor & Francis Group, an informa business

© 2019 Taylor & Francis

The right of Amanda Datnow and Vicki Park to be identified as authors of this work has been asserted by them in accordance with sections 77 and 78 of the Copyright, Designs and Patents Act 1988.

All rights reserved. No part of this book may be reprinted or reproduced or utilised in any form or by any electronic, mechanical, or other means, now known or hereafter invented, including photocopying and recording, or in any information storage or retrieval system, without permission in writing from the publishers.

Trademark notice: Product or corporate names may be trademarks or registered trademarks, and are used only for identification and explanation without intent to infringe.

Library of Congress Cataloging-in-Publication Data
A catalog record for this book has been requested

ISBN: 978-0-8153-4878-8 (hbk)
ISBN: 978-0-8153-4881-8 (pbk)
ISBN: 978-1-351-16588-4 (ebk)

Typeset in Adobe Caslon Pro
by Apex CoVantage, LLC

Contents

1	The Importance of Professional Collaboration	1
2	Collaborating With Purpose for Equity and Excellence	18
3	Collaborating With Professionalism and Coherence	39
4	Collaborating for Deep Learning	60
5	Collaborating Through Shifting Policies	78
6	Collaborating With Emotion	97
7	Leading Professional Collaboration	116

Acknowledgments	125
Index	126

1
THE IMPORTANCE OF PROFESSIONAL COLLABORATION

"Are we done yet?" This is a common refrain from teachers who feel forced into teacher team meetings that feel artificial or in which precious time is wasted. When we think about collaboration in the workplace, many of us can draw upon negative instances of when it *didn't* work. Anecdotes of collaboration time being used to tell "war stories," unstructured time without a clear purpose or agenda, and personality conflicts overtaking shared learning are all too familiar. If we have been fortunate enough, we can also recall deep and enriching joint work that led to purposeful growth and learning. Instead of minutes crawling by, time flies with engrossing discussions and collaborative practice, both of which have relevance to instructional decision-making and student learning.

Every teacher in every school deserves the opportunity to engage in professional collaboration aimed toward bolder and deeper learning for school improvement. This is not about finding ways to get teachers to "buy in" to so-called professional learning communities that embody none of the terms in the phrase (Vescio, Ross, & Adams, 2008). Often, they are not professional, nor are they learning opportunities, nor are they characterized by community. In part, this is because school improvement efforts and policies have framed teacher collaboration in technical-rational terms, ignoring the ways in which teachers feel either *compelled* toward or *repelled* by joint work. Many districts and schools have established teacher collaboration opportunities in order to support changes in teaching and learning, but these collaborative experiences often do not meet their intended goal. Although some teachers have transformative experiences by collaborating with others, a large number do not. And when positive instances of collaboration exist, they may not last.

In this introductory chapter, we establish why professional collaboration is critical at this time, more thoroughly explore what it is, and discuss how it can make a difference. Building on research and practice, we share the ways in which teachers are moved toward joint work because of the motivation, inspiration, and energy that they personally—and collectively—gain from collaborating to improve student learning. We explore how collaborative settings can provide a space for working through the inevitable challenges that accompany the changing nature of teaching in the midst of various forms of accountability across the globe. Collaboration can also be a vehicle for teachers to negotiate complex environments with shifting policies, changing student populations, and new social and political realities beyond the school. Professional collaboration can be transformational in schools if it is oriented toward equity and excellence, thoughtfully engages evidence on student learning, is embedded into day-to-day schooling practices, and is carefully sustained. Ultimately, moving toward bolder and deeper learning for school improvement is built upon harnessing the power of teachers to work together for equitable and excellent schools.

Professional Collaboration as a Key Reform Lever

In the past two decades, collaboration has been viewed as a critical lever for school improvement. Teacher collaboration, especially, is increasingly viewed as an essential ingredient for improving teaching and learning around the world (Harris, Jones, & Huffman, 2017). One longstanding assumption about its impact is that any activity that reduces teacher isolation will be beneficial, in part because it improves teacher morale (Little, 1990). Moreover, professional collaboration is predicated on the belief that teaching is a profession and that teachers have expertise, skills, and knowledge to drive their own professional learning and development (Campbell, Lieberman, & Yashkina, 2017). In theory, there would be equal emphasis on *professional* and *collaboration* in these efforts, with careful attention paid to the quality of collaboration that teachers are experiencing and the actual impact on students and school improvement. Actual practice varies, however. The press for teacher collaboration takes place in specific times and places, and implementation has evolved as educators have responded to broader accountability policies and public pressures to improve student achievement.

Although we talk about it as a monolithic entity, collaboration takes different forms in different countries, in large part due to differing perceptions of its value and the time allocated to it (Hargreaves & O'Connor, 2018; Jensen, Sonneman, Roberts-Hull, & Hunter, 2016; Kelchtermans, 2006). In contrast to the United States, where teachers average 27 hours of teaching per week, teachers in other systems spend anywhere from 10 to 23 hours per week on teaching, leaving more time for professional learning and development (Jensen et al., 2016). Collaboration activities have also been shaped by national and state accountability systems that have defined what school improvement goals are to be prioritized. In the United States, for example, policies driven by the No Child Left Behind Act of 2001 focused on increasing student achievement in math and English language arts, and critics believe that they led to a narrowing of the curriculum. This narrowing, not surprisingly, had implications for how schools structured their collaboration and, within these spaces, what counted as important data for continuous improvement. Furthermore, federal accountability policies focused on incentives, sanctions, and mandates, and this meant that schools faced high-stakes pressure to improve performance. Many schools and districts in the United States implemented professional learning communities (PLCs) to enable teachers to examine data on student achievement and to chart plans of action collectively.

In other countries, collaboration has taken different forms and served different purposes, often connected to national or local reform agendas. Just as in the United States, many countries expect that teachers will draw on evidence to improve teaching and learning (Stoll, Brown, Spence-Thomas, & Taylor, 2017). In Scotland, efforts to close the achievement gap have involved collaborative teacher action within and between schools (Chapman, Chestnutt, Friel, Hall, & Lowden, 2017). New Zealand is also promoting cross-school collaboration and has focused inquiry among teachers and leaders (Timperley, Ell, & LeFevre, 2017). In British Columbia and in England, networking teachers for inquiry has been integral to systemic educational reform efforts (Kaser & Halbert, 2017). Singapore has implemented professional learning communities as part of a systemwide and state-led initiative (Hairon & Goh, 2017). Ontario, Canada, has supported teacher collaboration systemically as well, but with more of a ground-up approach to incentivize teacher-led professional learning (Campbell et al., 2017).

As school improvement and accountability mechanisms evolve across the globe, how educators are able to practice professional collaboration is also shifting. In their book *Collaborative Professionalism*, Andy Hargreaves and Michael O'Connor (2018) talked about how the idea has evolved from Shirley Hord's (1997) conceptualization of professional collaboration for continuous inquiry, to DuFour's (2004) notion of PLCs, which emphasized teacher teams centered on student achievement, to its current iteration that broadens what counts as learning and collaboration as professional practice across the globe.

Hargreaves and O'Connor (2018) noted that the current generation of professional collaboration reflects five shifts in what is emphasized within collaborative practice:

1. From focusing on narrow learning and achievement to embracing wider purposes of learning and human development.
2. From being confined to episodic meetings in specific times and places to becoming embedded into teachers' and administrators' everyday work practices.
3. From being imposed and managed by administrators and their purposes to being run by teachers in relation to issues identified by themselves.
4. From serving the purpose of accountability to serving the needs of students.
5. From "comfortable" cultures to constraining structures and then to integrated structures and cultures that promote challenging yet respectful conversations about improvement.

(p. 101)

On the whole, these broader shifts represent an expansion of what counts as learning for both students and adults, driven by student needs that are holistically rather than narrowly defined. These shifts also reflect the understanding that to truly use professional collaboration as a lever for educational improvement, individual and collective learning must be integrated with practice as a day-to-day feature instead of ad-hoc or in weekly set-aside meetings.

In their study of professional learning in four high-performing systems (British Columbia, Hong Kong, Shanghai, and Singapore), Jensen et al. (2016) noted that "collaborative professional learning is built into the daily lives of teachers and schools leaders" (p. 4). More importantly, every educator is responsible for not only their own learning but also the learning of their colleagues. Collective learning and capacity building are emphasized. This is reinforced by reviews of international research, which suggest that effective PLCs exhibit key characteristics such as shared values and vision, collective responsibility, reflective professional inquiry, and collaboration (Kelchtermans, 2006; Stoll, Bolam, McMahon, Wallace, & Thomas, 2006; Vangrieken, Dochy, Raes, & Kyndt, 2015; Vescio et al., 2008).

There is also some evidence suggesting that professional collaboration, especially among teachers, can support positive student achievement (Goodard et al., 2010, cited in Ronfeldt, Farmer, McQueen, & Grissom, 2015; Saunders, Goldenberg, & Gallimore, 2009). Ronfeldt and colleagues (2015) found that "Teachers and schools that engage in better quality collaboration have better achievement gains in math and reading" (p. 475). In addition, the researchers concluded that quality professional collaboration can also lead to teacher learning and improvement: "Teachers improve at greater rates when they work in schools with better collaboration quality" (p. 475).

Several reviews of research on professional collaboration make it clear that not all collaborative practices are created equal, however. Studies examining qualities of teacher collaboration suggest that focusing on curriculum, instructional decision-making, and analysis of student data are more likely to promote student achievement gains (Ronfeldt et al., 2015; Vescio et al., 2008). Additionally, when there is frequent collaboration that is structured around inquiry protocols and student data and led by trained instructional leaders, teams are more likely to support improvements in student learning (Gallimore, Ermeling, Saunders, & Goldenberg, 2009; Saunders et al., 2009).

The Role of Data Use in Professional Collaboration

As practice and research continue to delve into how professional collaboration can support school improvement, teacher development, and student learning, data inquiry has become a necessary tool for understanding student learning needs and informing cycles of continuous improvement (Datnow & Park, 2014). Just like any tool for educational improvement, the use of data is constructed within a larger structure and culture and made sense of by individuals and groups that take part in professional collaboration. The literature on data use in schools offers a clear delineation between high-stakes, accountability-driven data use, which emphasizes complying with external pressures and bureaucratic demands, and data use for continuous organizational learning and improvement.

Firestone and González (2007) explained that an accountability-driven culture focuses on student test scores, tends to have a short-term time frame, and excludes teacher and principal voices. Data are used mainly to identify problems and monitor compliance. In contrast, they noted, data use for continuous improvement focuses on student and organizational learning and instructional improvement, is long-term in scope, and includes teacher and principal voices. Data are used to identify and diagnose problems. Educators who are focused on continuous improvement actively seek out a wide range of data and do not limit themselves to data linked to accountability mechanisms. The limitations of benchmark assessment data and teachers' interest in creating a more complete portrait of student achievement leads teachers to draw on a wide range of data to inform instructional decisions. The sources of data that teachers actually rely upon go well beyond these measures and include teacher-created assessments, curriculum-embedded assessments, writing portfolios, results from student work with online instructional tools, and of course their own observations of student learning.

When data are used during professional collaboration to foster inquiry, to critically examine instructional practices, and to identify opportunities to learn for both students and teachers, the information can be a useful tool for reflection and improvement (Horn & Little, 2010; Huguet, Farrell, & Marsh, 2017; Nelson, Slavit, & Deuel, 2012; Park, 2018; Schildkamp, Poortman, & Handelzalts, 2016). At the intersection of professional collaboration and data use, however, lies a black box with regard to how these practices actually unfold, evolve, and are enacted by teachers. We need a greater understanding of how teachers engage in professional collaboration with data use, taking into consideration not only the technical and procedural aspects of these practices but also the cultures in which they take place, the emotions they evoke, or the ways in which educators make sense of them. We have very few studies that "zoom in" on teacher practice (Little, 2012), and thus, despite the attention to data-driven decision-making in K–12 educational reform and policy, we know little about what teacher collaboration looks like in practice, especially with respect to the use of data. As such, key questions remain: What conditions support professional collaboration? And what role should data—or information on student learning more broadly—play in professional collaboration? This book helps to answer these questions and fill these gaps in our understanding.

Our Framework and Approach

In this book, we use in-depth empirical data to conceptualize professional collaboration. As described in Figure 1.1, to be purposeful,

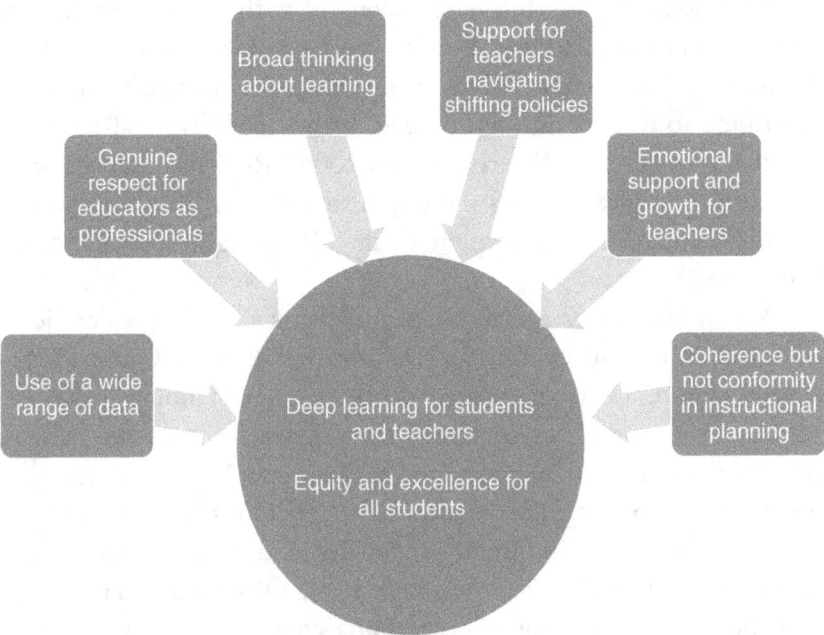

Figure 1.1 Purposeful Professional Collaboration: A Framework for Teacher Learning in Equitable and Excellent Schools

these efforts must embody a range of key qualities, from a focus on equity and excellence to respect and support for teachers as professionals and human beings.

We situate our work with the work of other scholars who believe in the potential of teacher joint work to foster meaningful improvements in teaching, learning, and equity. We adhere to a model of professional collaborative practice where both the notions of teacher professionalism and collaboration are equally emphasized. Borrowing from Hargreaves and O'Connor (2018), we define the professional aspect of professional collaboration as

> exercising good judgment, being committed to improvement, sharing and deepening expertise, and getting neither too close to nor too distant from the people the profession serves. The collaborative aspect of professionalism refers to how members of their profession labor or work rather than merely talk and reflect together.
>
> (p. 4)

We believe that talking and reflection are important aspects of collaborative learning, but this must be coupled with actions that directly lead to improving student learning and equitable outcomes. Furthermore, professional collaboration needs to be sustainable and not contribute to teacher burnout or lead to the deprofessionalization of teachers (Apple, 1986; Kelchtermans, 2006). Reforms aimed at collaboration can give teachers the impression they will be empowered, but in fact may serve to exploit them (Dillabough, 1999; Lawn & Ozga, 1981).

We consider coherence to be an important goal in teachers' joint work, but we do not advocate for conformity. Fullan and Quinn (2016) defined coherence as the shared depth of understanding about the nature of the work. They explained that alignment is not the same as coherence and argued for connected autonomy. Scholars who focus on the system are interested in uncovering what features need to be aligned to achieve coherence in initiatives, policies, and programs within and across schools (Hatch, 2001; Mehta & Fine, 2015), and also recognize that there are various routes to attaining coherence (Johnson, Marietta, Higgins, Mapp, & Grossman, 2015). Our notion of coherence aligns with these principles and focuses specifically on how coherence unfolds within professional collaboration among teachers rather than how coherence may be achieved across a system, important as this is.

Professional collaboration should provide opportunities for teachers to navigate through the emotional components of shifting policies, conflict, and change (Zembylas & Barker, 2007). Rather than being a waste of time or an emotional drain, professional collaboration should inspire, motivate, and energize teachers. In doing so, it can support deep learning for teachers and students alike. The conception of deep learning that is embedded in our definition of professional collaboration shares attributes with the broader system-focused notion of deep learning that Fullan and Quinn (2016) advanced, in that it is team-related, connects to teachers' passions, and has real-world significance. It is also both personal and collective. Shirley's (2017) notion of deep learning is similarly global and systemic in its reach. What we do here is bring to life deep learning and show how it can be found in the daily interactions of teachers who engage in professional collaboration. This micro-level, "on the ground" focus, we believe, will make deep learning a tangible possibility within teacher teams.

In some respects, our framework for professional collaboration is quite straightforward: Professional collaboration needs to *move* teachers in ways that promote equity for students, professionalism, coherence, and learning. In these ways, collaboration provides an important frame for teachers' work. At the same time, however, we acknowledge that engaging in professional collaboration is a complex initiative. Our perspective as researchers and educators is rooted in the assumption that professional collaboration and data use are socially constructed endeavors. In our previous book on data-informed leadership (Datnow & Park, 2014), we talked about the importance of the four Ps framework—people, practices, policies, and patterns—as a context-focused approach to understanding implementation of reform in schools.

We are obviously not the first to point out the importance of context. For example, Pak Tee Ng's (2017) recent study of educational transformation in Singapore also highlights how context and culture affect implementation. As a socially constructed practice, professional collaboration in districts and schools as well as within teacher teams is mediated by the people involved, as are the existing practices and patterns that are considered taken-for-granted norms and the school, district, state, and national policies that offer both supports and constraints. In other words, to understand the implementation of professional collaboration, we cannot simply look at school structures or team-based practices. Leadership plays a very important role in supporting and sustaining professional collaboration, and sensitivity to the local context is crucial (Vangrieken et al., 2015). In this respect, professional collaboration can be a rather delicate flower that needs to be carefully nurtured, protected, and accounted for in plans for continuous improvement. Meanwhile, little has been written about the sustainability of teacher collaboration over time (Stoll et al., 2006).

We also need to examine how social learning and cognitive capacity are built within schools. Learning is not solely a cognitive activity but also a socio-emotional one. We also assume that teachers engage in sensemaking both as individuals and collectively as a group, within teams, and across the school. Finally, we acknowledge that power and politics also come into play. In order to understand how professional collaboration plays out in a school setting, we seek to understand whose version of professional collaboration and data use are promoted or suppressed, and how teachers navigate some of these tensions.

For all of these reasons, professional collaboration is an emotional endeavor. Indeed, multiple emotional geographies comprise teachers' professional lives (Hargreaves, 2001). Teachers who work closely with each other can share emotional understandings and experiences, and moods can be infectious (Denzin, 1984; Hargreaves, 2005). When teachers value each other's expertise, have a common purpose, share responsibility for their students, and jointly problem solve (Little, 1990), they are bound together in professional emotional geographies as well as moral ones (Hargreaves, 2001). Emotions tend not to be examined in conceptions of teacher collaboration and yet, as we argue, emotions shape teacher collaboration and collaboration shapes teachers' emotions. While many positive benefits can be accrued, there is emotional work involved as well.

Our perspective recognizes what productive and positive collaboration looks like but also acknowledges the real challenges and hurdles that educators and schools encounter in making this vision an ongoing reality. Because schools and teams are in different stages of developing the capacity to engage in professional collaboration and are situated in different organizational contexts, we believe illuminating how educators strive toward this vision is important. Delving deeply into these issues requires ethnographic methods. Thus, over two years we conducted extensive observations and interviews in schools, taking a deep dive into teachers' collaborative work. We approached this work from a social constructivist framework, acknowledging that teachers' conceptions of professional collaboration and data use are produced in the course of their interactions with other teachers, administrators, and students.

We studied upper elementary grade teacher teams in four schools located in four different districts in the United States. Over a period of two years, we conducted extensive teacher team and classroom observations and interviews with teachers and leaders in these four schools, typically making biweekly visits. In total, we conducted 99 interviews, 180 hours of meeting observations, and 117 hours of classroom observations. We felt this in-depth work was necessary in order to answer these important questions about teachers' collaborative practices and data use and the conditions that shape them. Examining this empirical data in light of current research on educational change and teacher collaboration helped us build the conception of professional collaboration that we advance here.

Our knowledge base for this book is also supported by our interactions with educators, policymakers, and other researchers over the past decade. In addition to being researchers, we are also instructors of master's and doctoral students who are teachers and administrators in K–12 and higher education. We have taught courses that focus on or include research on data use and professional collaboration, and we have supervised doctoral students studying various aspects of school reform. We have shared our work on these topics with audiences from Oklahoma to Stockholm, in sessions with teachers, school and district leaders, researchers, and policymakers. Collectively, these opportunities have expanded our knowledge base on how data use and professional collaboration play out both in the broader policy sphere and within schools. We use this broad knowledge base, as well as our own reading of the literature, to inform the work in this book.

Structure of the Book

This book comprises a total of seven chapters. This beginning chapter has provided an introduction to the theoretical framework and empirical foundation that guided our work. Chapter 2 focuses on how professional collaboration needs to be purposeful with the goals of equity and excellence for all students in mind. Professional collaboration must be embedded within this larger vision. We discuss how an equity mindset coupled with high expectations for students is a necessary element of moving toward professional collaboration for teaching and learning. This equity mindset also requires serious consideration of the ethics that drive teachers' professionalism, which values schooling as a collective and public good. Purposeful professional collaboration requires clarity about the commitments to providing equal opportunities to learn for diverse students. Specifically, there are four key mindsets about students, learning, and collaboration that need to be shared across a school and cultivated by leaders: 1) All students are capable; 2) identifying student strengths is necessary to plan for student growth; 3) the needs of all students (not just a narrow band) must be considered; and 4) professional collaboration is about improving both student and teacher learning. In Chapter 2, we describe these mindsets and provide examples of how educators use them to guide their practices.

Chapter 3 presents the idea of collaborating for professionalism and coherence, focusing on the work of a teacher team that exemplifies these goals. Collaboration can cohere around a common set of systems for learning while preserving teacher professionalism both individually and collectively. Professional collaboration supports all teachers to engage in joint work that values everyone's expertise. This includes common goals for student learning, common processes for measuring student progress, and a shared belief in the power of evidence in informing instruction and school organization. The interdependence of a professionally collaborative team supports all teachers, develops new teachers, and promotes shared responsibility for student learning.

Chapter 4 explores how professional collaboration can lead to deep learning. Focusing on a case study of one school, this chapter takes a deep dive into collaborative practices and the use of evidence. We explain the allure of joint work for teachers who have the opportunity to delve deeply into what students should know and are able to do as well as how leadership supports these goals. We describe how collaborative structures focused on student-centered teaching and learning allow teachers the time and space to innovate. Engaging in an ongoing process characterized by genuine inquiry can energize teachers to generate unique ways of promoting and capturing student learning. In this way, professional collaboration looks very different from more typical, discrete-task-oriented teacher team meetings in which teachers superficially discuss student data under the guise of data-driven decision-making. Instead, professional collaboration focuses on what it really means for students to learn deeply, rather than simply "meet the mark" on externally imposed assessments.

Chapter 5 examines how teachers collaborate and navigate around shifting accountability policies and expectations. We explain how some teachers struggle to find common ground with their colleagues as the policy landscape continually changes around them, including what counts as student progress and meaningful instructional practice. In such cases, professional collaboration is about learning how to stand on solid ground and figuring out how to make teaching meaningful while dealing with rapid changes made by others. The frustrations that teachers face in the era of accountability and centralization, with standardized programs and assessments, are real and must be acknowledged. We describe how these challenges are dealt with and what efforts have been made to engage in productive joint work when teachers feel disempowered, context is ignored, and learning opportunities are few. This chapter underscores how, despite these challenges, striving to find value and inspiration in teachers' work is an essential core of professional collaboration.

Chapter 6 focuses on the role of emotions and how teachers collaborate with and through them. We discuss both the positive and negative emotions associated with professional collaboration. On the one hand, collaboration can support teachers emotionally, buffering them from external demands and the stress of reform. In this sense, collaboration can create collective resiliency. Collaboration can be a place of joint celebration of both student and teacher learning as well as a source of inspiration to try new ideas and get feedback on improving practice. When collaboration is productive, it can lighten the "burden" around curriculum design and instructional planning. On the other hand, there is emotional work associated with collaboration. It can drain teachers' time and energy—a large challenge, given that time is a valuable and finite resource. We explain how productive collaboration requires interpersonal skills to manage one's own and others' emotions—skills that are not necessarily always acknowledged or explicitly cultivated. Furthermore, there is danger to professional collaboration if groups are isolated from school and system. This can lead to "groupthink" or reinforce norms of contrived collegiality instead of professional collaboration for deep learning.

In the concluding chapter, we review the ingredients for professional collaboration and summarize key lessons for leaders in a set of clear and direct statements. We offer concrete, research-based suggestions for how leaders can support professional collaboration with teachers as co-developers in this complex joint work. Many paths can lead to improved professional collaboration. However, professional collaboration that moves toward equitable and excellent schools needs to center on teachers' learning development, motivation, and socio-emotional needs throughout their careers.

References

Apple, M. (1986). *Teachers and texts: A political economy of class and gender relations in education.* London: Routledge.

Campbell, C., Lieberman, A., & Yashkina, A. (2017). Teacher-led professional collaboration and systemic capacity building: Developing communities of professional learners in Ontario. In A. Harris, M. Jones, & J. B. Hoffman (Eds.), *Teachers leading educational reform* (pp. 88–101). London: Routledge.

Chapman, C., Chestnutt, H., Friel, N., Hall, S., & Lowden, K. (2017). Taking the lead: Teachers leading educational reform through collaborative inquiry. In A. Harris, M. Jones, & J. B. Hoffman (Eds.), *Teachers leading educational reform* (pp. 9–31). London: Routledge.

Datnow, A., & Park, V. (2014). *Data driven leadership.* Thousand Oaks, CA: Jossey-Bass.

Denzin, N. (1984). *On understanding emotion.* San Francisco, CA: Jossey-Bass.

Dillabough, J. A. (1999). Gender politics and conceptions of the modern teacher: Women, identity and professionalism. *British Journal of Sociology of Education, 20*(3), 373–394.

DuFour, R. (2004). What is a "professional learning community"? *Educational Leadership, 61*(8), 6–11.
Firestone, W. A., & González, R. A. (2007). Culture and processes affecting data use in school districts. In P. A. Moss (Ed.), *Evidence and decision making: Yearbook of the National Society for the Study of Education* (pp. 132–154). Malden, MA: Blackwell.
Fullan, M., & Quinn, J. (2016). *Coherence: The right drivers in action for schools, districts, and systems.* Thousand Oaks, CA: Corwin.
Gallimore, R., Ermeling, B. A., Saunders, W. M., & Goldenberg, C. (2009). Moving the learning of teaching closer to practice: Teacher education implications of school-based inquiry teams. *Elementary School Journal, 109*(5), 537–553.
Goddard, Y., Miller, R., Larsen, R., Goddard, G., Jacob, R., Madsen, J., & Schroeder, P. (2010). Connecting principal leadership, teacher collaboration, and student achievement. Paper presented at the American Educational Research Association Annual Meeting, Denver, CO.
Hairon, S., & Goh, J. W. (2017). Teacher leaders in professional learning communities in Singapore: Challenges and opportunities. In A. Harris, M. Jones, & J. B. Hoffman (Eds.), *Teachers leading educational reform* (pp. 86–99). London: Routledge.
Hargreaves, A. (2001). The emotional geographies of teachers' relations with colleagues. *International Journal of Educational Research, 35*(5), 503–527.
Hargreaves, A. (2005). Educational change takes ages: Life, career and generational factors in teachers' emotional responses to educational change. *Teaching and Teacher Education, 21*(8), 967–983.
Hargreaves, A., & O'Connor, M. T. (2018). *Collaborative professionalism: When teaching together means learning for all.* Thousand Oaks, CA: Corwin Press.
Harris, A., Jones, M., & Huffman, J. B. (2017). *Teachers leading educational reform: The power of professional learning communities.* London: Routledge.
Hatch, T. (2001). Incoherence in the system: The implementation of multiple initiatives in one district. *American Journal of Education, 109*(4), 407–437.
Hord, S. M. (1997). *Professional learning communities: Communities of continuous inquiry and improvement.* Austin, TX: Southwest Educational Development Laboratory.
Horn, I. S., & Little, J. W. (2010). Attending to problems of practice: Routines and resources for professional learning in teachers' workplace interactions. *American Educational Research Journal, 47*(1), 181–217.
Huguet, A., Farrell, C. C., & Marsh, J. A. (2017). Light touch, heavy hand: Principals and data-use PLCs. *Journal of Educational Administration, 55*(4), 376–389.
Jensen, B., Sonneman, J., Roberts-Hull, K., & Hunter, A. (2016). *Beyond PD: Teacher professional learning in high performing systems.* Washington, DC: National Center on Education and the Economy.
Johnson, S. M., Marietta, G., Higgins, M. C., Mapp, K. L., & Grossman, A. (2015). *Achieving coherence in district improvement: Managing the relationship between the central office and schools.* Cambridge, MA: Harvard Education Press.

Kaser, L., & Halbert, J. (2017). Teachers leading reform through inquiry learning networks: A view from British Columbia. In A. Harris, M. Jones, & J. B. Hoffman (Eds.), *Teachers leading educational reform* (pp. 32–50). London: Routledge.

Kelchtermans, G. (2006). Teacher collaboration and collegiality as workplace conditions: A review. *Zeitschrift fur Padagogik, 52*(2), 220–237.

Lawn, M., & Ozga, J. (1981). *Teachers, professionalism, and class: A study of organized teachers.* London: Routledge.

Little, J. W. (1990). The persistence of privacy: Autonomy and initiative in teachers' professional relations. *Teachers College Record, 91*(4), 509–536.

Little, J. W. (2012). Understanding data use practices among teachers: The contribution of micro-process studies. *American Journal of Education, 118*(2), 143–166.

Mehta, J., & Fine, S. (2015). Bringing values back in: How purpose shapes practices in coherent school designs. *Journal of Educational Change, 16*(4), 483–510.

Nelson, T. H., Slavit, D., & Deuel, A. (2012). Two dimensions of an inquiry stance toward student-learning data. *Teachers College Record, 114*(8), 1–42.

Ng, P. T. (2017). *Learning from Singapore: The power of paradoxes.* New York, NY: Routledge.

Park, V. (2018). Leading data conversation moves: Towards data-informed leadership for equity and learning. *Educational Administration Quarterly, 54*(4), 618–647.

Ronfeldt, M., Farmer, S. O., McQueen, K., & Grissom, J. A. (2015). Teacher collaboration in instructional teams and student achievement. *American Educational Research Journal, 52*(3), 475–514.

Saunders, W., Goldenberg, C., & Gallimore, R. (2009). Increasing achievement by focusing grade-level teams on improving classroom learning: A prospective, quasi-experimental study of Title 1 schools. *American Educational Research Journal, 46*(4), 1006–1033.

Schildkamp, K., Poortman, C. L., & Handelzalts, A. (2016). Data teams for school improvement. *School Effectiveness and School Improvement, 27*(2), 1–27.

Shirley, D. (2017). *The new imperatives of educational change: Achievement with integrity.* New York, NY: Routledge.

Stoll, L., Bolam, R., McMahon, A., Wallace, M., & Thomas, S. (2006). Professional learning communities: A review of the literature. *Journal of Educational Change, 7*(4), 221–258.

Stoll, L., Brown, C., Spence-Thomas, K., & Taylor, C. (2017). Teacher leadership within and across professional learning communities. In A. Harris, M. Jones, & J. B. Hoffman (Eds.), *Teachers leading educational reform* (pp. 51–71). London: Routledge.

Timperley, H., Ell, F., & LeFevre, D. (2017). Developing adaptive expertise through professional learning communities. In A. Harris, M. Jones, & J. B. Hoffman (Eds.), *Teachers leading educational reform* (pp. 175–189). London: Routledge.

Vangrieken, K., Dochy, F., Raes, E., & Kyndt, E. (2015). Teacher collaboration: A systematic review. *Educational Research Review, 15*, 17–40.

Vescio, V., Ross, D., & Adams, A. (2008). A review of research on the impact of professional learning communities on teaching practice and student learning. *Teaching and Teacher Education, 24*(1), 80–91.

Zembylas, M., & Barker, H. B. (2007). Teachers' spaces for coping with change in the context of a reform effort. *Journal of Educational Change, 8*(3), 235–256.

2

Collaborating With Purpose for Equity and Excellence

Like too many other school structures and reform strategies, professional collaboration has been treated as an end rather than as a means to an end. How can we tell? Schools that are on the professional learning community (PLC) bandwagon start with the structure and focus on planning in detail what the PLC meetings should look like, how frequently they should be held, which adults in the school building should control the agenda, and how much time should be allocated to each topic on the agenda. In these cases, the PLCs become another form of faculty meetings rather than a vehicle for learning together as a community of practice. To be clear, we are not dismissing the importance of attending to the management of structures; rather, we are troubled that the discussion of management often supersedes a larger discussion about the purpose and vision for professional collaboration that should drive decisions about time, frequency, and agenda. The focus becomes the cycle of doing and acting without the investigating and reflecting part. In these cases, PLCs exist only in name and not in purpose for teacher and student learning. Activities drive the process rather than the overarching goal (Bradley, Munger, & Hord, 2015).

If we are to treat professional collaboration as the means rather than the end, we have to seriously ask and be able to answer clearly, to what end? Yes, we want teachers to learn to improve their practices. But what are they learning for? And yes, we want teachers to collaborate thoughtfully. But again, what are they collaborating for? The ultimate goal of professional collaboration has to be centered on improving student learning and making sure that all students have equal opportunities to learn. Without this core value to anchor professional collaboration and school improvement overall, it can lead to "activity traps" where it becomes easy to equate *change* with *improvement* (Robinson, 2017).

Ensuring equity through equal opportunities to learn is an essential core of the collaborative endeavor. In conceptualizing equity, we borrow from Pollock's (2017) definition in her book, *Schooltalk*. Pollock defined equity as supporting the full human talent development of *every* student and *all groups* of students. In her conception, equity-oriented school talk is guided by principles of respecting all students' well-being, describing students accurately, pinpointing students' needs—precisely, not vaguely, and regularly, not rarely—and sharing opportunities to learn widely. Achieving equity in education involves genuinely providing equal opportunities to learn for all students and paying diligent attention at the macro and micro levels to how schools produce unequal processes and outcomes.

Large-scale accountability policies across the globe, and particularly in the United States, are often narrowly focused on highlighting student achievement gaps at the expense of understanding and mitigating the effects of unequal educational conditions and processes. Reform efforts have consequently focused on ways to close these gaps without necessarily examining the ways in which existing school cultures and structures contribute to creating them. We concur with Ladson-Billings (2006), who argued that the term "achievement gap" unfairly constructs low-income and minority students as defective or lacking and places the burden on them to catch up. Instead, using the term "education debt" moves us to a discourse that holds educators and policymakers accountable for providing students access to the educational resources that will allow them to achieve at high levels. It turns our attention to the conditions that can support and meet the needs of diverse student populations.

Ladson-Billings (2006) further advocated for deploying our best research knowledge, skills, and expertise to alleviate the poor educational conditions and learning experiences that students receive in many schools. If we are to seriously view improving student learning and equity as the central goal driving professional collaboration, then educators in a school system have to be able to answer for themselves:

What is good teaching and what counts as learning for both adults and children? How do we ensure that all students in the school have equal opportunities to learn and equal access to high-quality education? Whether we acknowledge it or not, our explicit and unspoken assumptions about learning and teaching will drive how we interact with our colleagues, what ideas we take up, and what practices we are willing to reconsider and act upon.

Mindsets for Purposeful Professional Collaboration

Instead of starting from a place of describing what productive professional collaboration for equity and student learning looks like, we deliberately start with making clear the mindsets that are needed for thoughtful practice. In our previous work, we talked about the importance of learning not just practices but principles that drive practice (Datnow & Park, 2014). That is because we know that practices are not always effective for every teacher or every student in every school.

Take the role of data discussion protocols. These are simply tools, neither good nor bad, either effective or ineffective, depending on the context. In a PLC meeting where teachers are novices at data discussions and desire facilitation support, such a tool can be helpful in providing some guiding structure for examining data and planning future lessons. This same data discussion protocol, when transported to another PLC meeting where teachers are used to discussing formative assessments regularly for lesson planning, might seem unnecessary or too constraining. In this context, data are a pivotal part of the discussion in the form of student work samples; the discussion is centered around the knowledge that students are able to demonstrate through their work rather than around the protocol itself.

In one school we visited, the administrative regulation that accompanied the protocols led some groups of teachers to focus on the tasks (e.g., completing a form describing the outcome of their discussions of data), rather than on meaningful discussions around data. In a data team meeting, the overall goal appeared to be making sure that all parts of the protocol were discussed with the 50 minutes allotted for the meeting. With the focus on form completion, teachers spent less time engaging in a deep discussion of instructional strategies needed to better support students. At the culmination of the meeting, one teacher filled in the last part of the protocol and remarked, "Yay, we're done! What time is it?"

In examples like this, we do not fault individuals or teacher teams or attribute how PLCs operate simply to them. Teachers' experiences and wisdom of practice matter in how they develop instructional improvement strategies. At the same time, leadership and school culture play critical roles in enabling or constraining their ability to do so. School leaders can help set the tone for data use among teachers, focusing them away from or toward accountability and equity concerns.

In Horn, Kane, and Wilson's (2015) study, one teacher work group's instructional management logic aligned with the principal's focus on accountability. They adopted his frame of data use as a monitoring activity rather than as a vehicle for examining students' mathematical understanding. There are also schools and districts in which leaders have strategically framed the use of data in an effort to produce more equitable learning opportunities and outcomes for all their students (Park, Daly, & Guerra, 2013). These leaders have constructed sensemaking frames centered on the need to confront disparities in opportunities to learn, school improvement as a shared collective responsibility, and making incremental structural and cultural changes to ensure sustainability of reform goals. The school principal and a coach in another school we studied redirected dialogue toward students' strengths rather than weaknesses and oriented the conversation around improving practice (Park, 2018). In these cases, we see a deliberate commitment on the part of leaders to frame data use for instructional improvement as an *equity-driven activity*.

Thus, leaders wield a great deal of power in shaping how professional collaboration does or does not happen. Beyond ensuring that there is time for PLC meetings, school leaders need to consciously and explicit shape mindsets about the purpose of professional collaboration. Principles and mindsets make up the framework by which practices are taken up and enable revision and adaptation based on context. When educators implement a practice, it is too easy to say it did or didn't work. Because it is true: It probably will not always work based on the intentions and goals of the practice and for all types of students. For instance, when a teacher says a reading strategy

Table 2.1 Key Mindsets in Professional Collaboration

1. All students are capable.
2. Identifying student strengths is necessary to plan for student growth.
3. The needs of all students—not just a narrow band—must be considered.
4. Professional collaboration is about improving both student and teacher learning.

---

doesn't work with her students, she probably means that using the reading strategy as she initially practiced it did not lead to improving all students' reading competency. If the goal is fidelity to implementation, then it may make sense for this teacher to discard the strategy altogether. If the goal is adaptation based on the needs of her students, then she gives herself space and time to adjust the practice and revise it based on student responses that she observes. Data, in the form of her observations of students and their reading assessments, are involved and inform her next instructional steps. But the mindset of fidelity versus adaptability is also at play. Her orientation toward her practice and her ability to adjust her practice as she enacts new ideas will determine whether ideas are discarded or improved upon.

If educators are to move away from activities driving outcomes toward purposes driving activities, mindsets for professional collaboration are key. Purposeful professional collaboration requires clarity about the commitment to providing equal opportunities to learn for all students. Specifically, there are four key mindsets about students, learning, and collaboration that need to be shared across the school and cultivated by leaders. In this chapter, we describe these mindsets and provide examples of how educators have used them to guide their practices.

Mindset 1: All Students Are Capable

In the United States, the No Child Left Behind Act of 2001 drew sharper attention to systemic achievement gaps among student subgroups based on race/ethnicity, income, special education needs, and English learner status. This policy continues through the current Every Student Succeeds Act. Although the language about "leaving no child behind" assumed that the educational system was responsible for ensuring that all students performed to high expectations, the reality is that beliefs about the capabilities of students based on ability and background remain an ongoing challenge for educators. Deficit beliefs about students of color, those who come from low-income backgrounds, and those who need special education services have historically shaped how teachers have taught and how schools have structured opportunities to learn (Valencia, 2010).

These differentiated expectations and structural opportunities are evident in the practice of tracking or streaming students into classes based on their perceived ability. The logic of tracking and static grouping often embodies a fixed orientation toward student ability and learning (Oakes, 2005). Typically, in this instance, ability is conceptualized as stable, unidimensional, and easily assessed (Oakes, Wells, Jones, & Datnow, 1997). From this logic, data are often used in a high-stakes manner that is evaluative of the student's intelligence. Supporters of ability grouping argue that it enables teachers to be more effective and efficient since they have a narrower range of needs to address; critics argue that ability grouping denies opportunities to those in the lower groups, who are often low-income students of color (Gamoran, 2011; Oakes, 2005). Ultimately, tracking and ability grouping are driven by values of efficiency and the goal of minimizing the diversity of learners in one classroom.

Beliefs and assumptions about ability are deeply held, both consciously and unconsciously. Starting with the mindset that all students can learn is more than repeating the phrase or espousing the belief. Moving beyond lip service means changing teaching practices and schooling structures and processes (Skrla & Scheurich, 2001; Skrla, Scheurich, Garcia, & Nolly, 2004). For professional collaboration, the mindset that all students can learn is reflected in how teachers talk about students, whether they are willing to challenge their pre-existing beliefs, and the instructional strategies they develop to meet the needs of diverse learners.

Paying close attention to teacher talk in the context of data collaboration meetings illuminates how teachers think about student ability, as teachers often discuss data in relation to individual student achievement. In our own work (Datnow, Choi, Park, & St. John, 2018) and in Bertrand and Marsh's (2015) study, No Child Left Behind and related accountability mechanisms have figured strongly into teachers' talk. Terms used to describe students, such as "low," "high," or "below basic," are reinforced by assessment data showing which students were below, at, or above grade level. These labels are imposed upon teachers by broader policies for accountability and have become part of teachers' lexicon. This lexicon appears to reify a hierarchy of ability and can constrain the ways in which teachers talk about student achievement and learning as well as their expectations of students.

When educators use student characteristics as explanations for results, they can reinforce a culture of low expectations and stereotypes (Bertrand & Marsh, 2015). For example, a teacher in Bertrand and Marsh's study discussed data on her students such that "the connection between 'resource kids' and the lack of proficiency was self-evident, suggesting an assumption that students in special education score poorly on tests by nature" (p. 19). Moreover, this teacher attributed the assessment results to her students, not to her teaching. The attribution of results to what were thought to be stable student characteristics was a pattern in this study, and English learners, special education students, and other struggling students were "blamed" for outcomes.

When educators use data to confirm deficit assumptions about student ability, this often goes hand in hand with comments about students' home lives being the primary explanation for student achievement. For example, one teacher we interviewed stated, "Go into the [district] website . . . and go take a look at the scores. You're going to find out that Asian kids score higher than White kids and Latino kids. And my experience is because of the discipline at home." When such assumptions are made, it is very difficult for educators to see data as a useful tool for improving their own practices or to perceive collaboration as a useful vehicle for professional learning, as they locate achievement patterns in their students' backgrounds, outside their locus of control.

At the same time, data use has been shown to be a powerful tool to push teachers to challenge existing assumptions about student learning and to reflect critically on instructional practices (Lachat & Smith, 2005). In one district, addressing teachers' low expectations for students who came from low-income families was a major hurdle. In our research, a principal had to explicitly persuade her staff that, "Yes, we have challenges, but our kids can do it. Now, look at other schools that are doing it, and comparing them, we can do it." The principal shared that teachers began to make the shift toward using data for instructional reflection when the school started to examine individual teacher data for their students, teacher attendance, and so forth. Schoolwide data were not initially useful in creating the shift toward viewing data as relevant for teachers. Furthermore, the shift did not occur smoothly. During the first year of the principal's tenure at the school, about 28 percent of the faculty left the school; about 18 percent left in the second year. The faculty was more stable thereafter.

In the same district, a school administrator explained that data had been powerful in changing teachers' perceptions about special education students. Over a period of two years, data showed that the inclusion of special education students in regular education classrooms was a success because many special education students could now perform at grade level. The administrator recalled that staff members initially expressed doubts about its success, however. Data played a key role in helping them admit that instructional strategies, not the children, were at the root of the problem of low student achievement. This belief shift was difficult. This leader believed that the first step in changing attitudes was building trust, so that teachers felt secure enough to come to a meeting and admit, "My kids are not learning and [to] ask how can you help me?"

To have a mindset that all students can learn is to ask and explore how the current learning system may not be meeting the needs of all students (Ladson-Billings, 2006; Santamaria, 2009; Skrla et al., 2004). This is reflected in the extent to which educators move away from locating student achievement gaps or learning needs to the individual level to examining how existing school structures, conditions, and processes may not be meeting the needs of diverse learners or denying students access to quality education.

One school that we studied reflected this purposeful focus on equity mindsets, especially by the leadership. Billings Elementary School serves a predominantly low-income student population from immigrant Latinx and Asian backgrounds. The new principal grappled with how best to support teachers to have growth mindsets about their students and about themselves (Dweck, 2010). She reflected on the structural and cultural elements that would ensure that teachers have high expectations of all students; she also wondered how to provide the necessary learning scaffolds and socio-emotional supports to the teachers themselves. She knew that schools were not set up to easily meet the needs of everyone, and she critiqued schooling conditions. At the same time, she explored alternative ways to structure learning for students and support teachers' development on this issue:

> It's something that I wrestle with in general. I kind of have this philosophical thing where I don't think schools are set up to educate everybody, and that's a shame. That's a real problem. So that's when I get really excited about exploratory learning. Those are the places where kids like Matthew, he's a second grader, he's just really hyper. If we do more project-based learning, if we do more exploration, if we do more real life experiential learning, he's going to buy in. So yeah, do I think he's challenging in a traditional classroom? I do. He'll yell out, and he's just really excited, and he'll ask, "Hey what's going on?" The other part is the structure isn't conducive to him learning. So how do I just slowly shift people into that kind of process, and then also communicate, "Here are the behavior things that you need to have in place." Because you need to set up structures. So that requires a lot more thinking as opposed to, "Okay, what's the basic parts of lessons I need to cover?"

In this quote, the principal acknowledged that traditional classrooms are not always set up to bring out the best in all children. She also thought about what it would take for teachers to make these changes. She was trying to shift thinking about structure, practices, and mindsets to accommodate different learners.

In sum, the mindset of "all students are capable" is more than a mantra. Practices and school culture intentionally translate these beliefs into concrete, everyday action. Enacting this mindset also means examining the conditions and processes that do or do not lead to student success. Examining data can help support this shift. More importantly, it is vital to this endeavor that teachers have the collaborative space to reflect on their instruction with data and that leaders set the vision to focus on equity and excellence. If everyone in the school truly believes that all students are able to learn, then the focus becomes, what can we do as a school or professional collaboration team to ensure that students are learning? Ownership of change and improvement is then placed with the adults in the school rather than with individual students or groups of students. This is translated into practice through professional collaboration focused on identifying student strengths and areas of growth, as well as consideration of students holistically.

Mindset 2: Identifying Student Strengths Is Necessary to Plan for Student Growth

The mindset that all students can learn needs to be coupled with the mindset that identifying students' strengths is critical to improvement efforts. Deficit language and mindsets are problematic not only because they locate failure or blame individuals but also because they do not lead to solutions or improvement strategies. A deficit mindset also does not account for existing strengths that could be used as a foundation for further improvement.

Educators who learn about Vygotsky often refer to the Zone of Proximal Development to figure out how to scaffold learning (Bruner, 1985). This developmental approach to learning focuses on understanding where the learner is currently situated and what it will take for the learner to get to the learning goal that stretches them but is achievable. The focus is also on how to scaffold students' learning so they are able to get to the learning target. Lily, a teacher at Billings, described why understanding and examining student strengths was so critical to scaffolding learning targets:

> For me, if I don't see their strengths in the beginning of the year I'm not even going to know how much they've improved at the end of the year. . . . Maybe they could just read a sentence and stop for that period and read another sentence. But their strength at the end of the year is, "Wow, they're decoding multisyllabic words, and they're doing [it with] expression."

As this teacher's mindset on student growth indicates, identifying student strengths isn't simply about telling positive stories. It is also not about patronizingly boosting student morale. Assessing student growth involves real information and data that are needed to scaffold and plan for student learning. Students' and teachers' strengths are the resources and the platform that enable learning to occur.

The process of closely examining data in the context of teacher team meetings can facilitate teachers' focus on student growth, thereby shaping teachers' beliefs about what they think their students are capable of. The team meeting can provide a space and a routine for teachers to point to various forms of "data" when making claims about student achievement. In our own work (Park, 2018), we have found that these opportunities for dialogue, with purposeful facilitation around data, can help teachers move away from deficit framing of students and toward discussions of specific student strengths and growth. Professional collaboration time is centered on reflecting on student learning—both what they know and where they need to grow.

Many schools already have PLC structures where student data are discussed for interventions or lesson planning. If structured with a protocol, teams are also primed to talk about student strengths and weaknesses. However, in some of the PLCs we have observed, there was a tendency to focus on student weaknesses and to discuss student ability in generalized terms (e.g., "the student is low" or the "student can't read"). When available, coaches or other instructional leaders can play a critical role in reframing conversations toward student assets (Park, 2018). For example, when a teacher at Billings expressed concern or frustration about "low students" or attributed low academic performance to ability or motivation, leaders redirected the conversation to also highlight the specific learning skills that students did exhibit. This can be as simple as asking a question like, "What did the student do well?" or "What skills has the student already mastered?"

If we are to take seriously the notion that student strengths are resources for learning to occur, teachers and administrators must get to know their students holistically. Students bring with them a wealth of experiences and knowledge that educators can use to build bridges to academic learning (Moll, Amanti, Neff, & Gonzalez, 1992). Schools serving low-income communities of color in particular must recognize and then build on the "community cultural wealth" (Yosso, 2005) that students and their families bring to school with them. In order to do so, educators must actively seek out opportunities to know their students beyond the classroom—their cultures and histories as well as the diverse ways in which their families contribute to their education.

Ben is a teacher at Billings, where many of the students are English learners. He acknowledged the challenges faced by his students but also believed that it was important to highlight their strengths:

> Our test scores, particularly in reading and writing, are low. When I hear the students talk, they've got great ideas, and I think it's an issue of confidence and experience using written English. I think our kids have lots of strengths, too, though. I think they're oftentimes emotionally resilient. I think a lot of them living in a low-income situation have been asked to do quite a lot at a young age and know that they're capable. I'm certain that the majority of my students feel really well loved by their families as well. They have really strong families from what I've seen. The parents that I've worked with, by and large, they really have high hopes for their students. And we try and work hand in hand with that.

In the end, data can play a very powerful role in challenging stereotypes and providing an opportunity for educators to examine the relationship between instructional practices and student learning. But simply deciding to build professional learning communities is not sufficient to bring about change. As Pollock (2017) argued, school talk must debunk myths about intelligence as easily measurable; it must explicitly challenge common comments about young people or families that are harmful. Framing conversations carefully and providing the opportunity for educators to bring multiple sources to bear on conversations about student achievement are critical. Furthermore, explicitly focusing on student strengths is a vital component of scaffolding student growth.

Mindset 3: The Needs of All Students—Not Just a Narrow Band—Must Be Considered

Under the high-stakes accountability system in the United States, studies have shown that educators, especially those serving under-resourced and under-performing communities, engage in "educational rationing or triage" (Gillborn & Youdell, 2000, cited in Booher-Jennings, 2005)—for example, by examining state assessment data to determine which students are on the "bubble" or cusp of grade-level proficiency and then investing resources to push these students over the threshold of the proficiency marker. Students who are very low performing are considered "lost causes," and those performing above grade level are not focused on either. This triage approach leaves many students behind. By focusing on the use of data to avoid sanctions, educators, whether intentionally or unintentionally, subvert the intended goal of these policies.

The focus on a narrow band of students can play out in different ways with different consequences. At one school we studied, an English language support teacher pulled students out for language support, and an intervention teacher pulled out the struggling readers in each class for small group instruction. As a teacher explained, this allowed her to focus on the bubble kids: "I kind of focus on the kids that didn't quite make it into that reading group, but still aren't proficient, so it's kind of the bubble kids. And it's a smaller group, so I can really focus in on the skills that they need to be proficient." In this school, educators were trying to use resources strategically to address the needs of a band of kids across all grades who were identified as "not proficient." More commonly, schools focus only on the bubble kids and leave the "just too low" ones behind (Booher-Jennings, 2005).

A focus on students on the bubble shows up not just in individual teacher planning, but in teacher conversations as well. Halverson, Grigg, Prichett, and Thomas (2007) found that faculty data discussions overwhelmingly centered on helping students below proficiency levels, with few discussions focused on raising students from proficient to advanced levels. While such practices may result in greater numbers of students achieving "above the mark," they inadvertently compromise the overarching purpose of data-informed decision-making, which is to expand opportunities for all students.

Shared responsibility can bolster professional collaboration because it creates a common goal. Within these shared learning spaces, a mindset of meeting the needs of diverse learners must be coupled with an instructional framework that is student-centered. The literature on differentiated instruction suggests that in order to meet the needs of all learners, we must broaden how we think about students' needs and students' demonstrations of their learning. In contrast to the logic of ability grouping, differentiated instruction is presented not just as a set of practices but also as a student-centered mindset driven by the principles of responsive teaching (Tomlinson et al., 2003). According to Tomlinson and colleagues, student needs should not solely be defined by results on assessment tests or academic ability levels but also by readiness, interests, and learning profiles.

With this larger perspective on student needs, the focus is on meeting individualized learning goals through flexible, relevant, and varied student supports including student grouping for instruction (Santamaria, 2009; Tomlinson, 2014). Some ability- and skills-based grouping may occur in the context of instruction, but it is not static or the primary means of meeting the needs of diverse learners. In certain contexts, within-class grouping for selected subjects is considered to be effective if instruction is carefully tailored to students' needs, if students remain in a heterogeneous setting for most of the day, and if the groupings are flexible (Slavin, 1988). Additionally, within this instructional model, formative and summative assessment, among other forms of information on student learning, are used for frequent monitoring of student progress and to inform instruction.

Within classrooms, teachers implement a range of student grouping and differentiation strategies. In the schools we studied, these decisions were often informed by a combination of curriculum-related tests, formative assessments, and teacher observations (Park & Datnow, 2017). Sometimes the groupings were deliberately homogeneous by skill area and other times they were heterogeneous. A teacher at Billings, for example, had a strategy for grouping students by skill area, and this process was driven by an assessment she administered:

> When I was looking at it [data from online reading assessments and class formative assessments] one of the students in my lowest group and in my highest group both missed 18 questions on cause and effect since they've started. So next week I'm going to use that to just group all my kids that need help on cause and effect, all my kids that need help on main idea. And they're going to be literally across the entire span of reading equivalency from second grade to eighth grade.

This one-time grouping was intended to be for targeted intervention around a specific concept rather than a static group based on ability levels in reading.

Meeting the needs of diverse learners requires thinking about the different ways students can demonstrate what they have learned (i.e., multiple types of and modalities of assessment). But more importantly, it requires teachers to adjust the content, pacing, and process of learning while also considering the climate of the learning environment itself (Tomlinson, 2014). These tasks are not easy. They necessitate deep planning and careful thought about pedagogy and classroom management. It is essential that teachers have the space and time to grapple with these issues and learn from one another as a professional community.

Mindset 4: Professional Collaboration Is About Improving Both Student and Teacher Learning

Improving student learning is the primary goal that drives meaningful and purposeful collaboration. But without an emphasis on teacher learning, it is hard to get there. In the beginning of this chapter, we talked about PLCs that become logistical meetings or discussions that focus on swapping stories. Neither of these types of meetings typically leads to changing teacher beliefs, learning new skills, experimenting with practices, or innovating instruction. Teacher learning is the essential vehicle by which student learning can be accomplished. Thus, teachers too need ample opportunities to learn, to experiment, and to develop learning goals.

A professional collaboration mindset founded on teacher learning requires consideration of how to support and scaffold the development of adult learners. It also necessitates thinking through how to provide space and safety to risk trying new practices where success is not ensured and a willingness on the part of teachers to be vulnerable about failing or not knowing all the answers. These shifts to learning mindsets take time to foster. They often start with empathy for students and a perspective that is formed through a student-centered lens. Marie, an instructional coach, described how this mind shift was being cultivated at Billings:

> I know with a couple of the teachers that are on that path, we've had many conversations about putting yourself in the spot of a parent of those children. What would you want for them? I mean, our staff is caring, and we're all at different places in our careers, but very caring. And so kind of trying to come at it from that lens. If that was your child, would

you want the teacher to try to do something to meet them at their level? What would you expect, and then how can we support you so that you can do that? I think for some of them it was just knowing that they don't have to figure it out by themselves. It's not a judgment on their teaching, but it is a practice that needs to be changed. So I think that for some of them, because they're ready to hear that, I think that has helped.

Developing and supporting a learning mindset did not come as a result of mandating change. Certainly, mandates may result in compliance but likely do not lead to learning. Learning is more than engaging in practice, although enacting practice is a key component. As Marie noted, acknowledging the need to improve is fraught with emotional peril for some educators, as they perceive it as a judgment about their abilities. Thus, it is helpful when there is a shared belief and value for continuous learning, as everyone is positioned as a learner. Furthermore, Marie noted that she reassures teachers that they do not have to "figure out" how to improve or support students on their own. This has the effect of positioning everyone as part of a community of learners.

This finding suggests that school leaders cannot shortchange the development of professional identities centered on learning. It also suggests that educators cannot take for granted that community simply occurs when groups come together. Instead, it must be deliberately fostered and reinforced through meaning making and identity development activities. Developing a learning stance within professional collaboration time means encouraging educators to ask lots of questions. Thoughtful questioning can lead to teachers engaging in inquiry and mulling over what it means to teach and to learn. When teacher teams need support in their shift toward a learner-centered identity, it is helpful to have models of what this looks like in practice.

The mindset of professional collaboration for learning was reflected in PLC meetings at Billings. There, teachers met as grade levels during their PLC time. Although facilitated by an instructional coach, the teachers drove the content and focus of the meetings, coming up with their PLC goals and student assessments. When we studied the school, Lily and Ben were working together with Vanessa, a special education teacher for the upper grades who joined them as a first-year teacher. During their third PLC meeting of the year, they took time to reflect on their goals and the progress they had made. They first discussed what had worked well and the patterns they noticed in teaching math, which was their focal area for this inquiry cycle. Ben shared that his students' understanding of place value had improved. He acknowledged, "In years past, I also didn't teach it as well." This acknowledgement and awareness of growth was powerful for him and for his colleagues. Rather than presenting himself as an expert or focusing simply on what went well, he reflected on what helped him improve, such as modeling from the coach.

The process of collaborating led this same team to dig deeper into what they wanted students to learn and how to best assess their learning. This took time, with some false starts and quite a bit of brainstorming. The following vignette illustrates how the process unfolded for this team during their collaboration time:

The team decided to focus their next PLC goal on student writing. They noted that students were strong editors but needed to strengthen their revising skills. They took the time to tease out the distinction between editing and revising before the coach prompted them to consider what they would use for their pre- and post-assessment. Ben thought it could be a specific writing prompt. He added that the assessment should not be about assessing their reading abilities, and thus he thought a prompt about their lives, something everyone could write about, would be good. In response, Lily asked, "Would that be more of a narrative? How do we make it more of an informational essay?" The group took some time thinking about this and brainstormed. Ben asked, "What do we want to see in the assessment? Organizing ideas or sentences?" Lily replied that it should be on revising and not writing a paragraph but rearranging sentences, editing out a sentence, adding in sentences or information. She suggested using pre-created sentence strips. They continued to discuss the pros and cons of going this route, including the logistics of having students work with sentence strips but also being mindful to not conflate the purpose of the assessment, which was revising, with reading and writing paragraphs. Lily also added that she didn't want the assessment to be about the students' ability to read directions. The coach asked Vanessa if she thought that this was something her students could do as well. Vanessa replied, "I think so, but I would have to modify some." She continued to share ideas about adding in some easy examples for her students.

This team asked thoughtful questions about what exactly they were assessing students on, the differences between revising and editing, and what elaborating would look like. They were trying to clarify these learning concepts among themselves. By engaging in a collaborative discussion about creating the assessment for their PLC focus, the process raised important questions for the teachers about what they wanted students to be able to do with regard to specific standards, but it also gave them an opportunity to think about lessons that would need to be scaffolded for students. In a way, creating the assessment led them to backward map their lessons. They were able to accomplish this through shared goals and shared learning.

Providing the space and time to ask questions, brainstorm ideas, and clarify the purpose of instructional planning and assessments is an investment in teacher learning and growth. This type of professional collaboration requires a mindset that is open to not having all the answers immediately and being comfortable with exploration of ideas and experimentation. Positioning teachers as active individual and collective learners necessitates that leaders consider teachers' development to build the capacity to engage in deep learning and to scaffold their growth.

Conclusion

The four mindsets for professional collaboration we outlined in this chapter are more than mantras. Rather, they are orienting beliefs and principles that drive actual practice and how educators interact with one another and with students. We detailed how these mindsets are enacted in practice and how they can inform interactions during professional collaboration. As educators promote and develop structures for teacher collaboration, they need to have these mindsets at the forefront and assess if their collaborative practices enhance, rather than hinder, the goals of equity and excellence.

Key Takeaways and Reflection Points

- **A belief in students' ability to learn is essential.** A genuine belief that all students can and will learn is a critical component of professional collaboration, and it must be embodied in talk and practice. Educators should consider the extent to which they and their colleagues actually hold this belief and how it is expressed in daily conversations. Leaders may need to purposefully shift the dialogue to foster this mindset.

- **Data that demonstrate students' strengths are an essential component of the work.** Explicitly and consistently identifying and examining student strength data to plan instructional scaffolding is an important step toward realizing equity goals. Do educators, as a community, believe that strength data are necessary? Do current data sources emphasize student strengths? If not, what sources should be added? How can current data sources be utilized to identify and nurture student strengths?
- **All aspects of the student experience must be explored.** When teachers and leaders examine data, discussions must go beyond examining individual or class achievement data to involve an examination of the processes and conditions that support or hinder school success, such as access to programs. It is important for educators to take an honest look at what forms of data they are considering and whether they enhance or limit their goal of providing equitable opportunities for all students. What additional forms of data should be gathered to provide a more complete picture of equitable education for students?
- **Collaborative time must be explicit and intentional.** Achieving goals of equity and excellence requires that leaders structure and develop space and time to encourage professional exploration and experimentation. This often means going beyond time set aside for professional collaboration. Leaders would be wise to consider how time is used and whether current characterizations of collaborative time would fit the descriptors of "explorative and experimental."

References

Bertrand, M., & Marsh, J. A. (2015). Teachers' sensemaking of data and implications for equity. *American Educational Research Journal, 52*(5), 861–893.

Booher-Jennings, J. (2005). Below the bubble: "Educational triage" and the Texas accountability system. *American Educational Research Journal, 42*(2), 231–268.

Bradley, J., Munger, L., & Hord, S. H. (2015). Activities vs. outcomes: The difference makes all the difference. *Journal of Staff Development, 36*(5), 48–58.

Bruner, J. (1985). Vygotsky: A historical and conceptual perspective. In J. V. Wertsch (Ed.), *Culture, communication, and cognition: Vygotskian perspectives* (pp. 21–34). New York, NY: Cambridge University Press.

Datnow, A., Choi, B., Park, V., & St. John, E. (2018). Teacher talk about student ability and achievement in the era of data-driven decision making. *Teachers College Record, 120*(4), 1–34.

Datnow, A., & Park, V. (2014). *Data driven leadership*. Thousand Oaks, CA: Jossey-Bass.

Dweck, C. S. (2010). Mindsets and equitable education. *Principal Leadership, 10*(5), 26–29.

Gamoran, A. (2011). Designing instruction and grouping students to enhance the learning of all: New hope or false promise? In M. T. Hallinan (Ed.), *Frontiers in sociology of education* (pp. 111–126). Dordrecht, Netherlands: Springer.

Gillborn, D., & Youdell, D. (2000). *Rationing Education*. Buckingham: Open University Press.

Halverson, R., Grigg, J., Prichett, R., & Thomas, C. (2007). The new instructional leadership: Creating data-driven instructional systems in schools. *Journal of School Leadership, 17*(2), 159–193.

Horn, I., Kane, B., & Wilson, B. (2015). Making sense of student performance data: Data use logics and mathematics teachers' learning opportunities. *American Educational Research Journal, 52*(2), 208–242.

Lachat, M. A., & Smith, S. (2005). Practices that support data use in urban high schools. *Journal of Education Change for Students Placed At-Risk, 10*(3), 333–339.

Ladson-Billings, G. (2006). From the achievement gap to the education debt: Understanding achievement in U.S. schools. *Educational Researcher, 35*(7), 3–12.

Moll, L. C., Amanti, C., Neff, D., & Gonzalez, N. (1992). Funds of knowledge for teaching: Using a qualitative approach to connect homes and classrooms. *Theory into Practice, 31*(2), 132–141.

Oakes, J. (2005). *Keeping track: How schools structure inequality* (2nd ed.). New Haven, CT: Yale University Press.

Oakes, J., Wells, A. S., Jones, M., & Datnow, A. (1997). Detracking: The social construction of ability, cultural politics, and resistance to reform. *Teachers College Record, 98*(3), 482–510.

Park, V. (2018). Leading data conversation moves: Towards data-informed leadership for equity and learning. *Educational Administration Quarterly, 54*(4), 618–647.

Park, V., Daly, A. J., & Guerra, A. W. (2013). Strategic framing: How leaders craft the meaning of data use for equity and learning. *Educational Policy, 27*(4), 645–675.

Park, V., & Datnow, A. (2017). Ability grouping and differentiated instruction in an era of data-driven decision making. *American Journal of Education, 123*(2), 281–306.

Pollock, M. (2017). *Schooltalk: Rethinking what we say to—and about—students every day*. New York, NY: New Press.

Robinson, V. (2017). *Reduce change to increase improvement.* Thousand Oaks, CA: Corwin.

Santamaria, L. J. (2009). Culturally responsive differentiated instruction: Narrowing gaps between best pedagogical practices benefiting all learners. *Teachers College Record, 111*(1), 214–247.

Skrla, L., & Scheurich, J. J. (2001). Displacing deficit thinking. *Education and Urban Society, 33*(3), 235–259.

Skrla, L., Scheurich, J. J., Garcia, J., & Nolly, G. (2004). Equity audits: A practical leadership tool for developing equitable and excellent schools. *Educational Administration Quarterly, 40*(1), 133–161.

Slavin, R. E. (1988). Synthesis of research on grouping in elementary and secondary schools. *Educational Leadership, 46*(1), 67–77.

Tomlinson, C. A. (2014). *The differentiated classroom: Responding to the needs of all learners* (2nd ed.). Alexandria, VA: ASCD.

Tomlinson, C. A., Brighton, C., Hertberg, C., Callahan, C. M., Moon, T. R., . . . Reynolds, T. (2003). Differentiating instruction in response to student readiness, interest, and learning profile in academically diverse classrooms: A review of literature. *Journal for the Education of the Gifted, 27*(2–3), 119–145.

Valencia, R. R. (2010). *Dismantling contemporary deficit thinking: Educational thought and practice.* New York, NY: Routledge.

Yosso, T. J. (2005). Whose culture has capital? A critical race theory discussion of community cultural wealth. *Race Ethnicity and Education, 8*(1), 69–91.

3

Collaborating With Professionalism and Coherence

Compared to other schools I've worked at, this is the school to be at, because the team collaborates for literally everything.

—Clarice, teacher

I wish every school in the world could have the team model that we do . . . Just talking to other teachers in the district, it's so sad to see some teams who are on an island.

—Hannah, teacher

These comments are from teachers working in a school that has a strong culture and structure supporting teacher collaboration. Why are schools like this so rare? What does it take for more teachers to have professionally rewarding collaboration experiences that truly fuel their teaching? Having a driving purpose of equity and excellence for all students, as we discussed in the previous chapter, can provide a driving purpose around which teachers can unify. But a unifying purpose sometimes isn't enough. Collaboration needs to support professionalism and coherence in other aspects of teaching as well.

Does this mean that teachers need to all do the same thing? No. Teacher collaboration can cohere around a common set of systems for learning while preserving teacher professionalism both individually and collectively. Coherence involves teachers coming together around shared expectations for students. The intent here is not for teachers to be in lock-step, as a prescribed curriculum might dictate, for example. Rather, the spirit of professional collaboration with coherence is that teachers share goals for teaching and learning. Professional collaboration supports all teachers to engage in joint work that values everyone's expertise. The interdependence of a professionally collaborative team supports all teachers, develops new teachers, and promotes shared responsibility for student learning.

In this chapter, we profile Chavez Elementary, a school that exemplifies collaboration with professionalism and coherence. We spent two years at this school, studying the work of a team of seven elementary school teachers from two grades. The team had common goals for student learning, common processes for measuring student progress, and a shared belief in the power of evidence in informing instruction and school organization. While unique in many ways, this team was not an island of excellence. Rather, it was nested in a supportive school structure and culture. Embedded in this case are important lessons for leaders who play a critical role in enabling teachers to collaborate with professionalism and coherence.

A Glimpse Into Chavez Elementary

Tucked away on a side street near the freeway, across from a low-income housing complex, sits Chavez Elementary. Although the building is growing old, it is well-kept and inviting. The principal, counselor, and numerous teachers are outside the school every morning, welcoming children and families. Parents living in nearby apartments can walk their children to school, while others choose to drive to Chavez from the far reaches of the school district boundaries. The wide draw has resulted in a student community that the principal described as, "very, very diverse," mixed by race, language, and socioeconomic status. Rachel, a teacher, explained:

> The majority of the kids come from loving families who work really hard, and a lot of them are just on survival mode. They're working two, three jobs; they're not always there at night. . . . And then you've got those families who, you know, their parents are college educated and have doctorates, and everyone in between.

Chavez Elementary wasn't always a draw for the community, however. Rachel said, "For a long time it was an underperforming school, and there were a lot of teachers who loved the kids but used a lot of their outside situations as an excuse why they didn't learn." Over a decade ago, a visionary leader led the transformation of Chavez into a school with high expectations for students and for teachers. Reflecting on this shift, Rachel added, "We found over the years that you can still hold them accountable and love them at the same time, and that they learn."

By the time we began our study at Chavez, it was well established as a high-performing school that surpassed its peers on student achievement measures. The original leader had since moved on to an external organization to help other schools engage in a similar process of transformation, using the lessons of schoolwide change that began at Chavez. Due to its excellent reputation, the school had a waiting list of students and a regular stream of visitors who wished to learn from their successes. We didn't know the school's strong reputation when we selected it for our study, but we quickly learned what was unique about teacher professional collaboration in this school. These features included:

- common goals for—and measures of—student learning;
- collaborative processes for supporting student progress;
- support for professionalism in collaborative spaces;
- collaboration across and within teams;
- collaboration on the fly; and
- candid and deliberative collaboration

We discuss each of these features in detail in the sections that follow.

The PLC team at Chavez included seven teachers, and we refer to them in this chapter by their pseudonyms—Rachel, Courtney, Pat, Kim, Hannah, Kayla, and Clarice. For easy distinction between the teachers and the principal, we refer to the latter simply as "the principal," rather than with a pseudonym of her own.

Common Goals for—and Measures of—Student Learning

Entering a classroom at Chavez, one sees students who find their seats quickly and who are focused on engaging in learning with each other and with their teacher. With 35 students, class sizes at Chavez are relatively large, but this is not uncommon in U.S. public schools. College pennants adorn the walls. A poster behind the teacher's desk says, "We are college bound. Where will you be going?" Instructional time is always used carefully at Chavez, and it is rare that students aren't focused on something that supports their academic and/or socio-emotional development. On this particular day in Courtney's classroom, students work independently on assignments geared around their "Personal Academic Goals" in language arts. In another classroom, Kim works with students in small groups on language arts goal areas they have in common (e.g., improving their understanding of informational text).

Many schools and systems purport to have shared goals, but at times it can be hard to find teachers who can articulate the goals, much less work collaboratively to achieve them. Chavez has an overarching goal of college readiness for all students. In order to achieve this, there is an explicit academic goal that every student will be proficient in reading, language arts, and mathematics. This measurable goal is commonly shared among all teachers and the principal, but the goals of the school are much broader than that. Teachers explain that student learning is the "focal point" of the school. While in theory all schools are about learning, at Chavez this goal is underscored and permeates everything that teachers do. A teacher said, "We're here to learn—that's first and foremost. And everything else . . . anything else that's able to be fit in is gravy." The teachers have pride in these shared goals. Courtney explained:

> We are going to take these kids and we're going make sure that for those hours that they're here at school, we're going make those the most productive hours of their day, and we're going make sure these kids learn. . . . We take a lot of pride in that, and I think every teacher on this staff feels the same way.

These goals and the common sense of purpose might sound lofty, but at Chavez they are operationalized in clear ways. The school has common processes for measuring student progress. The list of measures of student learning is widely circulated. Students in all grade levels complete benchmark assessments in language arts, math, reading, and spelling as well as an on-demand writing assessment and a district math assessment. Is this a lot of assessments? Yes. But they are used for formative rather than evaluative or compliance purposes, which is unusual. At Chavez, teachers see the value of each assessment, which is something we don't often see in schools. Teachers believe that data are essential to guiding their instruction. Rachel explained:

> How is [data] going to guide your instruction? And how do you build your groups, and what does your day look like because of the data that you have? I mean, for us, it's very impactful. I don't structure my day, I don't know what I'm going to teach until I have that data in front of me.

Of course the use of data could be an entirely individual endeavor. At Chavez, using common assessments has allowed teachers to be "on the same page" when talking about kids. Again, the goal is not for them to teach the same material in the same way, but rather to cohere around a set of standards and agreement around how progress toward those standards will be measured. Teachers co-created their own assessments based upon their beginning, middle, and end-of-year standards. Again, Rachel explained:

> We've come up with our own assessments that we're going to use, so that then we have a common language, and we know what we're talking about. So that when we get in the meeting it's not like apples and oranges. . . . We're coming in with the same set of data and the same set of information so we can have those meaningful conversations about the kids.

At the school and classroom level, data from these assessments drive a process of class- and individual-level academic goal setting for students. Initially, teachers used data to set specific goals with each of their students in reading, language arts, and math, but this was very overwhelming for the staff. After a few years, they decided to focus only on creating reading goals with students because, as Pat noted, "Kids come in struggling more as readers than they do in language conventions or math." Rachel's reflections are once again useful:

> We set a class goal first, and then what we do is we look at their lowest area. And based on my knowledge of [their assessment scores], and also them as a student, we determine together what their goal is going to be.

And then once we've determined what the goal area is, I'll pull that group and we'll set up a goal for them. Then they have to take some ownership of it. They will decide, with my guidance, what they're going to do to meet that goal.

Kim clarified that while the whole class read the same novel, she met with the student groups "related to their goal work." She continued:

So there might be one group that's working on a lot of vocabulary development within the story, one group that was doing more literal comprehension and genre specific work with it, some that were doing interpretive comprehension, and some that were just working on more literature-response-analysis-type activities based on their needs that were demonstrated through the testing.

Hannah explained, "One of our favorite sayings is, 'a goal without a plan is nothing but a wish.'" Thus, the teachers shared a common belief that the student plays an important role in influencing his or her own success. This is achieved by students setting their own goals. In a fourth-grade class we observed during goal-setting time, Courtney said to the students, "If I am a runner and I want to get better at my race time, what do I do? I could eat better, run more often, etc. So now we decide what we have to work on in order to get better. These are our action pieces." She explained to the students: "This group is going to be working on informational text, which is our non-fiction reading. You're all very strong in reading, but this is the one area that you are going to work on."

At some schools, goals for student learning and ways of measuring progress can become stale over time. Years later, when educators revisit them, they seem out of date. At Chavez, however, goals and measures are revisited by the leadership team, which includes teachers, every year. The school has one-page documents describing what collaboration, assessment, and data analysis "look like" at Chavez. "Every year we rip it apart," the principal explained. "This is what we had, does it still look good?" Once the revisions have been made, the team comes together to say, "this is what we endorse" and "we're going to hold each other accountable for it," she added. She mentioned that these statements were not "in a binder that sits on the shelf. It's something that's live, and we work with it."

Collaborative Processes for Supporting Student Progress

> *I do think our school is unique in the fact that we really do use data . . . The other thing that I think makes us unique is that we're not afraid to share our data with each other.*
>
> —Rachel, teacher

A shared belief in the power of evidence is foundational to teacher collaboration at Chavez. But believing in evidence is not enough. Teachers need to work collaboratively to support student progress. Data can be an important part of this process, but data don't drive it, nor should that be the case. Educators need to thoughtfully engage with each other in elevating the educational experiences of all students. This process takes a particular form at Chavez, and one that is relatively unique even in schools that purport to be data-driven.

Educators at Chavez have long engaged in a comprehensive process of data analysis three times per year. This process has involved grade-level teams of teachers (e.g., two grade-level teams), two or three intervention teachers (including an English learner support teacher), a school counselor, and the principal getting together for two hours to examine data on every student served by each team of teachers. Teachers are provided with substitute release time to attend.

As we sat down to join one of these meetings, we quickly noticed that the meeting routine was very clear to all participants. The tone was purposeful and professional, yet there was evidence of a friendly rapport among everyone in the room. They talked easily among themselves and genuinely seemed to work together well in trying to address student needs. The teachers led the discussion, raising issues about each student one by one. But the principal, counselor, and resource teachers also chimed in continuously.

The purpose of these meetings was to discuss student progress, assign students to interventions, or adjust flexible ability group placements in English language arts. This happened within a month of the start of the school year, in winter, and in the spring. At the spring meeting, the group also discussed classroom placements for the following year. While serving these goals, the meetings also allowed teachers to openly share data on all of their students, which then allowed for a discussion of the strategies that would best meet students' needs. Having teachers from two grade levels at these meetings helped to promote interdependence, as teachers were not focused only on students in their own classes or even grades.

To prepare for the meetings, the school's data clerk organized student data, enabling the team of educators to discuss each student and their performance on various assessments as well as how they were doing more generally. Participants were provided a spreadsheet that included data on every student in the grade levels being discussed. The team examined a wide variety of data on student achievement, including a range of assessments, interventions, or other designations (e.g., English learner), all of which appeared on a single sheet, listed by student. In addition to the spreadsheets that were provided by the data clerk, the group also accessed other data on the district's data management system. Occasionally, a member of the group would access the system to look up patterns of student attendance, assessment data dating back several years to see if there was a trend over time, or even a student's birthdate to see if a student might have been particularly young for the grade (which could explain classroom behavior, etc.). As the principal noted, the goal was to figure out "what might be hindering the learning for students and trying to get past those barriers." Even at a beginning-of-the-year meeting, all of the adults in the room seemed to know almost all of the students, except for those who were new. In their analyses of data, the group paid particular attention to increases and decreases in student performance because, as the principal explained, "We want to be sure that if they scored high or low in one particular area and it seems to be a fluke, we have other assessments that we can kind of tease it out to see was this just a bad day or is this where they really are?" Pulling together an array of data on each student in a single location was critical to this process.

The conversations took different forms depending on the students' progress and needs. In one meeting, Kim described one of her students: "In class when I talk to him, he seems to get it. But every time there's an assessment, he tanks it." She explained this even occurred with a quick quiz, such as an exit ticket in math. She noted that his interim assessment score was "the same as third grade," and he was now in fifth grade. The group discussed the student for a while and decided he needed extra support in math via pull-out instruction. When such an intervention was planned, teachers carefully considered what class time might be missed and how that might impact students individually or collectively. Problem solving often had to take place as teachers had to "think outside of the box," as one teacher described, when it came to addressing students' needs holistically. The group considered various support models, including having a resource teacher "push in" to work with small groups in the classroom.

Even though many data points for each student were made available, teachers did not believe that numbers, especially achievement measures, were the sole or most important data worth discussing. We sat in on many such meetings at this school and noted that educators were not just "chasing the numbers." Rather, in order to meet the needs of each child, educators engaged in a multi-dimensional evaluation of students' achievement, behavior, lives in and outside of school, and work habits. As the principal said, "Because we are not only talking about this number, that number, that number, we are talking about, [we are] just pretty open about what might be hindering the learning for students."

Table 3.1 describes the range of data that we observed teachers using to inform instruction at Chavez. Although many of these data points were listed on the data sheets, some were not but were occasionally referred to by educators in the course of their holistic conversations about how to meet students' needs.

Table 3.1 Data Contributing to a Holistic View of Student Achievement

- Standardized assessment data
- Benchmark assessment data
- Student attendance data
- Background information about students
- English learner designation
- Special education designation
- Teacher-created assessments
- Online program assessments
- Curriculum-embedded assessments
- Writing portfolios
- Classwork and homework
- Teachers' observations of students
- Student surveys or self-reflections

In addition to relying on many forms of data, relationships were critically important to teachers' decision-making about how to best support students. Teachers made it their business to know each other's students and their students' families. When one teacher shared a challenge related to meeting a particular student's needs, others shared information or teaching strategies that might have been useful. The meetings consistently reflected this holistic orientation to discussing students. Likewise, when educators collaborated to examine student data, they held each other accountable for meeting the needs of all children. Kim explained, "I think there has to be buy-in, that we're here to serve the whole community. I think when you have that common purpose, it really helps."

Support for Professionalism in Collaborative Spaces

Leadership played an important role in valuing teacher professionalism and expertise at Chavez. The data-focused meetings that occurred three times each year did have a particular agenda; in other collaborative spaces, however, the agenda was not set by administration. This is somewhat uncommon, as we have often observed overly prescriptive agendas dominate teacher discussions in other schools that purport to use data. Rather, the principal allowed the teachers to use their collaboration time in the ways that best suited their needs.

There was early dismissal once a week to provide teachers paid collaboration time. One afternoon a month was dedicated to faculty meetings, but teachers used the other afternoons flexibly. When the school first began its transformation years ago, agendas were structured by that administration, but with input from the teachers. However, over time it made more sense for teachers to plan their own agendas entirely. "We've been doing it for so long . . . we don't take advantage . . . I mean, when we have time, we're going to use our time," Rachel explained.

Relying on faculty judgment to guide these meetings, the principal explained, "It depends on really the time of year, and the time of the month, as to what's going on. Sometimes they might be just teaming to plan, sometimes to assess. You know, it just depends." Courtney corroborated this point:

So it really is very flexible. And our administration gives us the flexibility of how we meet. There's just the expectation that you are meeting, you're talking about plans, you're talking about kids. But we do have the flexibility of what it is that we are meeting about.

The principal explained that initially teacher collaboration time was "tighter" in structure. The administration made the move to less structured time because they wanted "collaboration time to be deeper, stronger [and] really just take our collaboration, which is already amazing, to that next level." Rachel explained:

Okay so what's our focus this year, and what are we going to concentrate our collaboration time on? What do you see as a need? It was rarely ever, "Hey, here's what we've decided, now go and do it. And whether you see value in it or not, too bad," which was always nice. We collectively came together and decided what we were going to do.

Rather than the principal establishing the agenda, the teachers used email to jointly develop it for each team meeting. The meetings addressed a wide range of topics such as curriculum standards, instructional practices, or assessments. Hannah explained, "Every time we do sit down we are always making sure that we're making progress in an area. So we kind of set a goal before we sit down, and then we make sure that we're hitting [it]. So the [meetings] are always very productive." This time was viewed as extremely valuable. Courtney added, "We all crave that time to get together" and said she missed it when scheduling issues, such as report cards or school breaks, got in the way. "Don't mess with our time together," she said.

Collaboration Across and Within Teams

Policies supporting teacher collaboration time are one attempt to address the isolation that many teachers experience. The flexible teacher meeting time was critically important to professional collaboration at Chavez. However, prior research reveals that collaboration time alone is insufficient to produce the successful and meaningful joint work that reformers are aiming for (Kelchtermans, 2006; Little, 1990; Stoll, Bolam, McMahon, Wallace, & Thomas, 2006). Other structures must also be in place to support these goals. Likewise, a culture that supports learning from each other must be in place: "To keep this school running well . . . we need to take care of each other at our grade levels," explained Pat.

Teacher collaboration structures at Chavez were designed to support dialogue within and across grade levels. This was facilitated by the use of various horizontal and vertical collaboration structures. At times the team we studied met as a full team across two grade levels; other times, teachers met in subject areas, in dyads, or by grade level. The teachers felt that meeting in these different formations was critical to their work, but they acknowledged it was not always easy to do. As Courtney explained, "There's so many different configurations, and figuring out how to get to those configurations in a timely, efficient way is probably the biggest struggle."

Teachers at the two grade levels intentionally teamed together in order to foster mentoring and sharing of expertise, as the teams included both veteran and new teachers. While the two newer teachers had an assigned district mentor for beginning teachers, Hannah noted that they were much more likely to turn to their immediately available teammates for advice and problem solving. She was struck by how different her experience was in relation to her counterparts at other schools: "It's amazing to get the perspective of some of my peers that are second-year teachers, and they're at more affluent schools. And I thought, 'Wait, what? You don't meet every day and talk about planning or talk about a kid or . . .?'" Similarly, Kayla explained how the collaboration structures at Chavez helped her successfully acclimate to her new teaching assignment:

> This is my third year here, and I started as a new teacher in third grade. And I didn't feel like I was on my own. I didn't feel as though they said, "You're teaching third grade—good luck!" I had my team where they said, "Okay, this is how we assess for reading, this is what we do for our assessments, this is what Chavez does, so here you go."

Experienced teachers viewed mentoring more junior teachers within the team as an important part of their profession. Rachel explained:

> We sit down, and we spend a lot of time with new teachers and/or new team members. Because even as you [move from] grade to grade . . . things change. And so we spend a lot of time helping new teachers figure out all that stuff.

Bringing in a new member of the team was an occasion to articulate principles and practices, providing opportunity to make implicit practices and beliefs more explicit: "We've been on the same page for so long, so it's been nice to have those conversations," she added.

At various points in the year, teachers engaged in vertical collaboration across a wider range of grade levels. A goal of vertical collaboration was to create coherence in student learning and to align expectations. Kim clarified the purpose in relation to math:

> I think our hope for those is to look at the conceptual understanding, such as how are we really building this fraction knowledge over the years. My hope, as a fifth-grade teacher, is that the more consistency there is, the easier it will be down the road.

Hannah explained what they might say to a colleague: "Here are things we're noticing in fourth grade that we expect them to be proficient in, and they're not. Or . . . what are you guys doing that's making their number sense so good?" The focus was on learning about what was working well while also ensuring that teachers from other grades were aware of the gaps in student preparation.

Kayla explained that these cross-grade conversations were facilitated by bringing in student work samples: "We got in vertical teams to kind of analyze what papers looked like at different grade levels, to kind of get that perspective, and really focusing on the positives of what sort of math knowledge is the student demonstrating through their work." She found this process to be "really powerful" because teachers were able to see how their colleagues approached teaching math concepts and what successes they had. This led teachers across grade levels to share lessons with each other online, via a Pinterest board that they created. Kim explained that it perhaps "seems silly" to use this medium, but it was very beneficial for teachers to see how others had approached certain topics so they could share strategies.

Collaboration on the Fly

More than two decades ago, Andy Hargreaves (1994) presented a helpful typology that differentiated among varied forms of teacher collaboration. These forms ranged from "contrived collegiality," in which teachers worked together in administratively controlled ways, to more genuine, deep, inquiry-based collaborative activities, and every variant in between. In the verve to support teacher collaboration, many school systems have created contrived spaces, in which collaboration is limited to overly regulated set-aside time. Quite simply, this is not going to produce teacher collaboration with coherence or professionalism. Teachers need to work together far more often—and of their own will—to produce this kind of collaboration.

In order to have coherence, a once-a-week meeting is insufficient. Collaboration must exist across time and space. Teachers at Chavez often used the term "on the fly" to describe their frequent, informal collaboration. As one teacher stated:

> A lot of it ends up being conversations on the fly—you know, in the hallway, in the lunchroom . . . particularly between partner teachers because we see each other so much that we kind of save what needs to happen just between our two classrooms for our own time.

In fact, Chavez teachers didn't really distinguish between formal and informal collaboration because it all happened so fluidly. Clarice said, "We meet at least two to three times a month to discuss what we're all on the same page of. And luckily, during lunch, a lot of the times things come out, and then we all end up collaborating there on the spot too." Collaboration was also motivated by the need to address ongoing issues as they arose. Clarice added, "Okay, what's the problem? Let's fix it." Informal collaboration allowed for collaboration in real time that could inform daily instruction. Courtney summed up, "Pat and I talk daily about what's going on in our classrooms, and sometimes it's at 9:00 at night, and sometimes it's on Sunday afternoons. I mean, we're in constant communication."

Kayla explained that she'd email her colleague and say, "Hey, can I meet with you? I'm just struggling on how to teach this division strategy to these kids." Similarly, Hannah said she would contact Kim and say, "'I don't know what I'm doing here.' Or, 'This seemed to be really easy for my kids.' Or, 'This seemed to be really hard for my kids.' Or 'What lessons are you skipping? What lessons are you modifying?' So that collaboration piece was huge." Rachel talked about bringing her data to Pat to get help problem solving: "Pat and I will sit, and I'll share data with him because a lot of times he knows the kids as well as I do. So it'll be, 'Okay, look, I have . . . you know, this one and this one. I can't figure out why it is that they're not getting this,' or . . ."

The high level of trust and respect among Chavez teachers allowed them to feel at ease in sharing challenges. Collaboration didn't just provide a "cup of comfort" as Hargreaves (1994) put it. Rachel elaborated:

> It's nice to have the stability and know each other's strengths. And to be able to, especially in all this change, be able to go and trust the people you work with, where you can say, "Look, I am messing up on this. I don't know. I need help in this area," or whatever, and to be comfortable to . . . do that. Because a lot of schools, you keep it within your four walls, you know, if you're struggling or something. And here that's not the case.

Having an "open door" climate in which teachers felt comfortable accessing each other's expertise was critical. At times data were connected to these help-seeking moments. Rachel explained, "I would go to [an intervention teacher] and I would say, 'Hey, I have Kelsey, [and] her fluency is 46 words per minute. I've tried everything. I don't know what else to do to help her. Do you have any suggestions?'" Teachers gave countless examples of cases in which they would go to each other for support in how to best meet students' needs. "Your room extends beyond these four walls," Rachel explained; she noted that she could go to her colleagues or to her principal for help and not fear that they would think less of her. She added,

> I think that happens slowly over time, and through examples, and by really, truly having people come in or having an open door where I can go to them and say, "You're an expert in, you know, whatever, . . . in reading or comprehension; I'm having trouble with this student, I need help . . ."

Teachers also relied on each other to manage new curriculum expectations. We observed this when the school began implementation of the Common Core State Standards in math. They discussed adaptations that were necessary, given that many Chavez students were English learners and may have needed support in meeting the language demands of the new math problems. Teachers used both formal and informal collaboration opportunities to work through some other challenges. As Courtney explained,

> There was a lot of discussion, every unit . . . What should be our emphasis? How are we going make the assessment worthwhile so that it gives us information, gives the kids information, and assesses actually what and how we are teaching?

It is important to note that the teachers' valuing of each other's expertise was also evident in how they organized instruction at Chavez. Teachers rotated students for various subjects, and this sharing of the same students provided many opportunities for shared dialogue. Within and sometimes across grade-level teams, teachers departmentalized for math, science, and social studies. All teachers taught language arts, and students were grouped based on data and thus were mixed across multiple classrooms. These groups were fluid and were re-evaluated throughout the year. This arrangement hinged on the fact that teachers were confident in each other's knowledge and skills. As Hannah explained,

> When I hand them off to Kayla or Clarice, I have to know that they're going to do the best that they can for that child, and vice versa. When they give me their kids to teach math, or reading, or writing, or whatever it is, they have to trust that I'm going to do the best I can for that child.

Notably, not only did the teachers at Chavez feel comfortable sharing students, but they also felt comfortable having their own children in each other's classes. All of the teachers we interviewed who were parents sent their children to the school. Capturing the sentiments of several of her colleagues, Courtney said, "My own kids are here, and I think that's the best endorsement you can give."

Strong informal and personal relationships supported the culture of collaboration. As Hannah said about their teammates:

> We always go and eat lunch together. It's not as if we're working through lunch. We make sure that we have that time too, to celebrate what's going on in our lives and talk about your kids or . . . "What are you doing this weekend?" So we're friends, I would say, as well—not just teammates.

Clearly for the teachers at Chavez, the professional benefits of informal and formal collaboration went well beyond positive interpersonal relations. This is relatively rare, as teacher teams often struggle to "balance personal support with hard-nosed deliberation about present practice and future direction" (Little, 1990, p. 520). However, the instructional decision-making at Chavez was informed by a structure and culture of evidence, which helped enable this to occur.

Candid and Deliberative Collaboration

By now it should be abundantly clear that collaboration was carefully woven into teachers' work at Chavez. The principal reported a very collegial working environment among the teachers, noting, "one thing about this staff is the collaboration is like none other." While this was cultivated over time, hiring collaborative teachers was also acknowledged as an important factor. Hannah explained, "the hiring process is really where it begins . . . You just felt this sense of belonging." She added, "If you're not going to be a team player, I mean, this is not the school for you."

Although some teachers believed that hiring the right people was the "magic sauce" in collaboration, others felt it was the principal's leadership. "I think if you are really trying to turn around a school that is not collaborating at all, I think it has to start with the leader. And I think it starts with a very bold, drastic statement," noted Courtney. By this she meant, "This is the direction we're heading. And if you're not on board, or you know that right away, here is our district's transfer paperwork, and I'm sure that you will be able to find something elsewhere."

Once teachers were on board, finding productive ways to address problems when they arose was an important part of keeping the collaborative culture functioning. The principal described a practice called "candid collaboration" in which teachers were encouraged to come together to engage with colleagues about problems in candid and supportive ways:

> We do have problems, we do have very typical challenges, struggles, problems. But one of the things that we do is we don't vociferate over it. We just say, "Okay, this is how it is. What are we going to do?" Very solution-focused, very forward thinking, not a lot of griping at all, not a lot of back and forth. And . . . if somebody does kind of move into a more negative mode, we have what's called candid collaboration, where we . . .

in a very supportive manner, we do kind of get you where you need to be. And that's for everybody.

This was described as sort of an "intervention" approach where a small group might approach a staff member who they thought was struggling with something personally or professionally. This was not limited to teachers and also involved those in other roles at the school.

We found a great deal of consensus among the teachers, and instructional planning across each grade level and rotating students among their classes were commonplace. While teachers at Chavez did work harmoniously, they were comfortable disagreeing with one another when needed. Rachel explained that they disagreed "respectfully" and that, "it makes us all better teachers because we disagree, and we're comfortable disagreeing with each other." Occasionally teachers presented conflicting points of view about a student and eventually came to agreement about how best to characterize the student's achievement as well as how to support him or her.

When observing a team meeting, it was common to see teachers at Chavez engaged in a healthy, respectful debate related to the craft of teaching. During one meeting, the team's goal was to calibrate the scoring of students' writing assessments. The students had written essays in response to a prompt provided by the district. After jointly reading a student's paper, Pat provided this opinion: "That's not a grade-level piece of work." Courtney argued with this summation, pointing to evidence in the paper and to the rubric. She said, "There are glimmers of a 3," which is a score indicating that the writing meets grade-level standards. The team debated the merits of the student's work for a while, presenting different points of view. Eventually they reached consensus that the student's writing was not at the grade-level standard. They also had a lively discussion about the standards and critiqued the rubric they had been provided by the district, noting it reflected end-of-year standards rather than those for the beginning of the year, which is when the conversation took place.

These team conversations, which sometimes included initial disagreements and questioning, provided Chavez teachers with opportunities to collaboratively deliberate about their own understandings of what students should know and be able to do. Looking carefully at student work was an important ingredient, as was teachers' own comfort with their professional knowledge that allowed them to advocate for their positions while pointing to evidence. These occasions gave them the chance to push each other as professionals while ultimately cohering on common ground.

Conclusion

The Chavez case highlights the benefits of professional collaboration around a common purpose and teaching with measurable goals. A principal or district administrator might read this chapter and decide to provide flexibility to teachers in how they use their collaboration time and to lead them in developing common goals and implementing common planning time and three-times-a-year data analysis meetings to monitor individual student progress. Taken as a group, these structural supports can positively impact routines for teacher collaboration, but there is no guarantee, particularly if they are not accompanied by another set of shifts in conceptions of teachers' work. These less-tangible elements are the belief systems, norms, and working relationships among teachers and between teachers and the principal. Communicating trust is an important role for leaders. Collaboration with professionalism and coherence requires a mind shift in how we think about teaching and how teachers think about their colleagues. This is not to say, however, that structural supports are not important.

It is also important to underscore the fact that coherence does not mean uniformity. The role of the leader is to help teachers come together around common goals for teaching and learning. Teachers need space and time to work together, but they also need a leader who will support them in doing this work—work that is not only ongoing but also labor intensive. It is critical that leaders promote teacher collaboration around multiple forms of evidence on student learning, as we have noted elsewhere.

Key Takeaways and Reflection Points

- **Coherence is an important element of professional collaboration, but it cannot exist in a vacuum.** It must exist within a broader structure of coherence, or else teachers will feel they are working at cross purposes. Routines also need to be in place to allow teachers to jointly develop this coherence within their teams. Leaders would be wise to ask themselves, to what extent are the structures (e.g., time, space, facilitation support, flexibility) in place to support professional collaboration with a goal of coherence?

- **Evidence of student learning must be routinely examined and acted upon.** Such a routine is integral to professional collaboration. At the same time, it is much more challenging to develop routines that are authentic and do not involve simply "checking the box" of being data-driven. Taking a hard look at the structure supporting data use is essential for leaders and teachers alike.
- **Leaders need to communicate and model the valuing of multiple forms of evidence.** Careful framing of the culture around data use supports professional collaboration. Moreover, it is vital to take a holistic look at student development so that data use within collaborative settings doesn't become simply an exercise in compliance and accountability. Asking teachers to brainstorm the forms of data they find useful in creating a portrait of student achievement can be very useful.
- **Trusting relationships can be slow to develop yet are a foundation for professional collaboration.** Leaders and teachers both contribute to the development of trust. It is useful for both parties to consider, how is trust communicated in the ways that collaboration is organized and in how it unfolds?
- **Leaders and teachers should consider their own comfort level with and trust in the school.** An important litmus test for trust and the level of professional collaboration is to reflect upon whether leaders and teachers would feel comfortable sending their own children to their school. If the answer to this question is no, then it is wise to ponder how professional collaboration can help move toward this goal.

References

Hargreaves, A. (1994). *Changing teachers, changing times: Teachers' work and culture in the postmodern age.* London: Cassell.

Kelchtermans, G. (2006). Teacher collaboration and collegiality as workplace conditions: A review. *Zeitschrift fur Padagogik, 52*(2), 220–237.

Little, J. W. (1990). The persistence of privacy: Autonomy and initiative in teachers' professional relations. *Teachers College Record, 91*(4), 509–536.

Stoll, L., Bolam, R., McMahon, A., Wallace, M., & Thomas, S. (2006). Professional learning communities: A review of the literature. *Journal of Educational Change, 7*(4), 221–258.

4

COLLABORATING FOR DEEP LEARNING

We have observed many task-oriented teacher team meetings in which teachers superficially discussed student data under the guise of data-driven decision-making. In such meetings, administrators typically provide teachers with data on external assessments along with a set of questions to answer. Teachers often feel rushed to complete the form, leaving little time for reflection about the data or consideration of the implications for practice. This is not effective data use, and it certainly is not professional collaboration. Professional collaboration involves considering what it really means for a student to learn deeply, rather than simply "meet the mark" on externally imposed assessments (Hargreaves & O'Connor, 2018). Professional collaboration focuses on deep learning for teachers and students alike. Joint work can be alluring for teachers who have the opportunity to delve deeply into what students should know and are able to do. Collaborative structures focused on student-centered teaching and learning allow teachers the time and space to innovate. Engaging in an ongoing process characterized by genuine inquiry can energize teachers to generate unique ways of promoting and capturing student learning.

In this chapter, we profile a teacher team at Dewey Elementary School that exemplifies collaboration for deep learning. We spent two years at Dewey studying the collective work of a group of teachers through regular observations of team meetings, interviews, and classroom observations. Our research at this school also involved learning about the role of leadership in supporting deep teacher inquiry, which is where our story begins.

A Glimpse Into the Principal's Office at Dewey Elementary

The principal's office at Dewey Elementary looks like many others. Professional books on education line the bookshelves, the desk is neat and tidy, and there is seating available for the parents, teachers, and students who visit. The principal had a long career in public education, moving her way up the ranks as a teacher, teacher leader, assistant principal, and then principal for more than a decade. Along the way, she has furthered her own education. Her path into the principal role is not atypical. However, a closer look into her work reveals the important role that that leadership can play in supporting deep learning for teachers. At Dewey, this occurred through three primary drivers:

- differentiated teacher support;
- encouraging teacher teams to set their own professional learning goals; and
- fostering innovation.

Differentiated Teacher Support

Just as students need differentiated instruction, teachers need differentiated support for their professional learning. The principal recognized that the individual teachers and teacher teams in her school needed varied kinds of support depending on their professional learning goals, levels of experience, and working relationships with each other. She endeavored to find growth opportunities that would build on teachers' unique strengths and needs, departing from the typical approach of providing a one-size-fits-all model of teacher support.

One of the principal's core beliefs was that teachers need regular opportunities to be inspired by each other, and this helps them develop their teaching expertise. She motivated teachers to share practices by creating opportunities for them to observe in each other's classrooms: "I want them to be able to see others because I know it will be motivating and inspiring to see, 'Wow, that's how somebody's doing that.' And it causes them to seek out independently to be with that teacher." She planned for these observations to occur when instruction was happening, but also when it wasn't. In those cases, the principal asked teachers to observe evidence of learning that was visible. She explained that following observations, she "looked for the initiative of people who came to me and said, 'You know what? When I was in [a teacher's] classroom, I was really fascinated with this and this.'" She then arranged for the teachers to spend time learning from each other. She added, "And it doesn't create a competitive thing, it just helps them." She believed her teachers had a great deal of expertise and was eager to find ways for them to share wisdom with each other.

The principal used her own observations as a tool to support individual teacher development. She had different approaches for newer teachers and for those who had already honed their craft. She said that for newer teachers, "You'll see me really focused on an element that was very successful, and then a piece of instruction . . . that wasn't working as well." She would then have a discussion with the teacher about what could be done differently. When she met with teachers who already exhibited a great deal of teaching expertise, she brought in ideas for specific instructional strategies related to content because she wanted them to get feedback on both; for newer teachers, she explained, "it really will be around what wasn't there and what was there," instructionally speaking.

Dewey had a strong record of student achievement. As such, unlike in many other schools, the principal could not frame the need for instructional improvement for her teachers in terms of improving student results on traditional measures. She explained, "When you do have those very high standardized test scores . . . so your kids are doing well, it is more challenging for me to keep helping teachers raise the bar of knowing what they don't know." The goal was instructional improvement that pushed all students to achieve at high levels. As she said, "Our house isn't on fire, but we recognize that we have to be really clear about what the instructional shifts are." As her statement suggests, the focus was on implementing innovative instructional approaches that would deepen learning for students and for teachers.

Encouraging Teacher Teams to Set Their Own Professional Learning Goals

> *I'm very collaborative. I'm direct with individuals when I need to be, but the whole thing is that I want them to get there on their own. That's my style of leadership and that works for 95 percent of my teachers.*
>
> —Principal at Dewey

When it came to collaboration, the principal typically gave teachers freedom to set professional learning goals and met with them in the ways that worked best for their team. For example, one team might work on developing common assessments that would promote critical thinking in mathematics while another might develop proficiency-level indicators in reading. However, the principal provided an overall school goal, which was to figure out more concretely what students should know and be able to do to meet grade-level standards.

District policy mandated that schools dismiss students early once a week to allow for 90 minutes of paid teacher "PLC time" that could be used for collaboration. PLC time was used once a month for staff meetings led by the principal, and periodically the time was used for district professional development activities or to convene teachers across schools. This schedule typically left grade-level teams of teachers with at least two formal teacher collaboration meetings each month, although this varied. Teachers at this school also benefited from additional collaboration time when their students were in physical education, music, or other enrichment classes. In order to facilitate collaboration, the principal tried to schedule these classes at the same time of day for all students at a particular grade level. The principal recognized that teachers needed time and space to think creatively:

> I expect my teachers to be extremely thoughtful. I expect them to be intellectual about their work. It's very complex work. And so when you're doing that, I need them to be thoughtful . . . I expect them to create thinkers, and so I expect you to be a thinker. . . It's very intellectual, and you have to be really bright to do this work. And you have to be in the moment and you have to look for patterns and trends and figure out what you're going to do.

Teachers appreciated the autonomy in their collaboration time, as well as in their instructional practice. As one teacher explained:

> We've always had a lot of autonomy. I mean, we really have. The one thing that the expectation has been that we PLC with each other, we look at student work, that we set goals, and that we meet them as teams. That has always been a really big thing . . . It's about the kids making gains and having proof that what we're doing is working.

Another teacher explained her ideal PLC: "For me it would really just look like them blocking off time and turning us loose—no strings, no report back afterwards and tell me what standards you discussed, but just trusting us to do our work."

The principal recognized that teams had different strengths and approaches to working together, and she valued this diversity. She explained that one team might be more inquiry-based, focusing its time on sharing and reflecting on instructional strategies, whereas another might be more focused on working together to create assessments and reflecting on the products of student learning. Other teams might work together in different ways as well. She embraced the varied ways in which they approached their joint work, as long as it focused on improving teaching and learning.

The principal offered more structure to the teams she felt needed it and less structure to those who did not. She explained that the PLC model could look very different depending on the level of inquiry within a team:

> It can be very tight: Here's your data, here's your protocol, here's the steps you go through, or you get in each other's classrooms and here's the specific "look-fors" I want you to look for. And how loose and tight I am with all that stuff evolves based on the teams. And so trying to structure . . . so it's tight enough so they know what my expectations are, but loose enough to be able to meet the needs of all the teams.

She also realized that different teams might make more or less productive use of time. Teachers appreciated the fact that the principal recognized that some teams would benefit from more flexible or tighter guidelines for what would be accomplished in collaborative time. Not surprisingly, teacher teams at Dewey delved into discussions of student learning in a variety of ways. The principal described some teams as very strong in their efforts at working together and others as developing in their expertise at collaboration. Some teams were established, whereas others were newly formed or had experienced changes in key members. She attempted to support teams in the ways that best fit their needs.

Fostering Innovation

Knowing that teacher teams were at different levels in their collaboration and in terms of their own experience, the principal thought carefully about how to foster innovation among her staff. In addition to the aforementioned strategies of differentiated teacher support and encouraging teacher teams to set their own learning goals, she fostered innovation by providing resources for teachers and teacher teams who showed initiative in experimenting with new curricula or pedagogical strategies. She explained, "I give resources out a lot on initiative. Sometimes teachers here say, 'Well, why did they get this group of books or you allocated resources?' I said, 'Because they asked. They came with a plan and an idea and they asked. Go for it.'" This was not just the principal's stance, it was a value in the district as well. A teacher reflected, "So everything's about, 'What are you willing to try?'"

Numerous teachers were actively piloting new innovations in their classrooms and sharing their results with teammates and providing feedback to the principal and the district. At times, teachers were invited by district leaders to experiment with new teaching modalities or curricula. In these cases, as a teacher explained, the district mantra appeared to be, "Let's just choose people that are strong in their own classrooms and then the rest will come." Sometimes whole teams were chosen for district pilots. In these cases, teachers believed the strength of their collaboration also played a role in being chosen. As one teacher said, "We function very well with social capital, and I feel like that's a big part."

A Case of Collaboration for Deep Learning

We had the privilege to study a highly collaborative team at Dewey that comprised three mid-career teachers—Carla, Ella, and Marcia—who had taught together for several years by the time our study began. In the course of the instructional day, these teachers moved fluidly between each other's classrooms, touching base with each other as students moved between their rooms. The team regularly met informally, outside of established teacher collaboration times. As Carla explained, "We plan together for those to all kind of stay in the same genre, I guess. And then we also all really like each other, so we want to meet and work together. We're just a high-functioning team or a well-functioning team." The teachers often reflected on how lucky they were to be part of such a strong, united team, and they realized that colleagues at other schools were more isolated. Ella reflected on their strong ability to collaborate, seeing it as somewhat intangible: "It just kind of is a chemistry." She added, "I don't know if it's luck that our dynamics are such, but I'm truly amazed." They saw their positive team dynamics as directly contributing to their individual strengths in classroom teaching. "I feel as though we're one step ahead," explained Ella.

Elements of Deep Learning in Professional Collaboration

What characterizes a team that is "high functioning"? What do "high-level conversations" look like? How might we know deep learning among teachers when we see it? Once again, the experience of teachers and leaders at Dewey provides valuable insight.

Engaging in a collective process of inquiry energized and motivated this team of teachers at Dewey to generate creative ways of promoting and examining evidence on student learning. One of the teachers described the team's conversations as "meaty." The following vignette, from an observation during the team's collaborative time, provides a sense of what this means:

> *On this particular day, a grade-level PLC meeting was taking place in one of the teacher's classrooms. We quickly noticed that the teachers in this team were very comfortable with each other and swiftly moved into a rich conversation about instruction as PLC time began. The prompt for this PLC meeting asked teachers to focus their dialogue on an open-ended question: "Looking ahead to the next unit of math, what are the standards and skills your students will need to know and be able to do? What will the students do, make, say, or write to*

demonstrate their understanding of each?" This prompt was intended to engage the teachers in a dialogue of the substance and evidence of student learning. They had a full 90 minutes to work together.

The prompt provided by the principal loosely structured the conversation—the teachers did talk about math, but they only briefly glanced at the prompt. This freedom was welcome and helpful. The team discussed a recent math assessment that Marcia had developed and given to all of the students in the grade. The team rotated students for various subjects, and thus only Marcia taught the core math content. Carla provided additional math enrichment one hour per week. The fact that not all teachers taught math did not constrain their conversation, as they shared a collective interest in supporting their students' math achievement.

The assessment included a rubric at the top of the page. There were five questions total on the test, and they included complex thinking problems such as: "Ms. D wrote the number 58,637. Ms. J wrote the number 25,109. How many times greater is the 5 in Ms. D's number than the 5 in Ms. J's number? Use pictures, numbers, or words to demonstrate your reasoning."

Marcia, the teacher who had given the assessment, told Ella and Carla that she was "really worried" about the students who scored poorly. She told her colleagues the names of the students who fell in this range. She also pulled out a particularly low-performing student's test, and the teachers looked over it and reviewed the errors together. They agreed that the errors revealed fundamental misunderstandings of the concepts. The decided that lower-performing students would benefit from individualized instruction.

Marcia then showed her colleagues the reflection form that accompanied the test. This form is a tool in which students use test results as the basis for self-evaluation and reflection of their strengths and weaknesses. Students, who were referred to as "mathematicians," were asked to label their mistakes as "simple mistakes," "tricky," "didn't know," or "skipped." The students then responded to a prompt that said, "This data tells me that I can push myself by _____ (fill in the blank) and praise myself by _____." The goal was for students to identify how they could help their own learning of this particular math standard. At the bottom of the page was a challenge problem for students to solve if they wished. The use of language around mistakes and referring to the students as mathematicians was important, as it framed learning in a certain kind of way.

Reflecting on the students' results helped Marcia "know where the kids are at," as she explained. It allowed her to guide Carla, who provided math

> support as well: "Now I can tell you, can you meet with this group on this concept?" In the course of this conversation, which allowed the teachers to dialogue about how to use evidence on student learning to inform instructional decision-making, Ella reflected and said, "Your approach is helping me figure out how to do our content differently." Ella and Carla deferred to Marcia to give them guidance on what she would like to see the students know and be able to do in math. They viewed her as the math expert, and when other subjects came up, such as science, teachers then referred to that person as expert. Ella pondered whether the demands of knowing the Common Core standards were so great that this strategy would be useful for other teams as well.

As is evident in the vignette, Ella, Carla, and Marcia spent a great deal of time thinking about how to foster student learning and develop students' identities as mathematicians and being thoughtful about how to support each other's development as teachers.

In addition to some of the obvious elements, such as trust, rigor, and a focused dialogue on instruction, this team was unique in several other key ways that defined them in terms of deep learning. Deep learning in professional collaboration embodies the following characteristics:

- Teachers are on the same page figuratively but not literally.
- Teachers think broadly together about evidence on student learning.
- Teachers have critical conversations about curriculum and pedagogy.
- Teachers aim for continuous improvement and embrace innovation.

On the Same Page Figuratively, Not Literally

In many schools, there is an assumption that a goal of collaborative work is for teachers to cohere around common materials and practices. However, in a deep learning team, teachers share ideas, but there isn't an expectation that they will do things the same way. In essence, team members are "on the same page" figuratively rather than literally. As one teacher explained, "We're all on the same page in terms of our expectations for our kids." Ella elaborated:

> It's not as if we sit and say, "Okay, Monday at 9:00 we're going to do this and this." So basically I feel like when we meet, we discuss, "Okay, we're

doing opinion writing," and then we kind of all say, "This is how I'm doing it, this is how I'm doing it." We share that way. We are all really individuals on the same page. Does that make sense? You know, I've been on teams where it's everybody's doing the same worksheet, everybody's doing the same lesson, and I don't feel as though we're like that at all.

Ella was excited about the opportunity to learn something new from her teammate who might be doing something differently: "I'll walk in [to another teacher's] room and say, 'Oh my gosh. What are you doing?!'" She continued, "I have never done it that way and so I'm still really learning. It's crazy. Yeah, we're definitely not cookie cutter, but on the same page." The teachers respected each other's differences and still maintained unity.

Common expectations for students helped to orient deep learning among teachers. They had high standards for themselves and for their students. Underlying the educators' shared sense of responsibility for meeting students' needs were common beliefs about high expectations for students and for themselves as professionals. Trust was also a key component of their relationship. Just as we described with the team at Chavez Elementary, teachers on this Dewey team felt their students were in good hands when they went to other teachers' classrooms. Ella said, "It's a really good feeling when you send your kids away."

Thinking Broadly About Evidence of Student Learning

Deep learning for teachers is impossible in an environment where student learning is defined in terms of a single measure. There needs to be room for teachers to define student learning itself—as well as how it's measured—in varied ways.

Defining what constituted different levels of mastery of the Common Core standards (e.g., What does it mean to be at grade level? What does it mean to exceed grade level?) occupied this team's work for the better part of a year. The principal explained that the team was digging into questions like, "What is it a kid should know and be able to do?" She added, "It's hard work, but it's the right work." Ella pondered, the "standards are so broad, and what does that look like to be 'secure'? What's expected in the first trimester? Second trimester? Actual behaviors so that we could measure that." The work of this team informed the work of the district committee that was focused on fleshing out the standards. However, as Ella said, the professional learning they gained from doing the work themselves was formative: "It's easy to have somebody give it to you, but it's different when you've made them."

Ella, Carla, and Marcia valued different forms of evidence about student learning. By focusing on different aspects, they complemented each other. Ella explained:

> I think on our team Marcia is the person who is very data-driven, and she is an absolute data collector. That's how her mind works. I think Carla and I are more similar in that we do a lot of data collection, but it's so much more on just kid watching . . . We'll watch their body language. That's part of our data collection . . . We also really stay in tune with what's going on in a child's family, because that's how she and I function—more on that emotional level, which is one of the reasons why we end up being such a great team. We're all bringing different things to the table.

The teams were able to value different forms of evidence because this was valued by school and district leadership. Marcia explained that there was a "change in mindset so that now everything we do counts." She was referring to formative assessment, which was a big push in the district during the time of our study.

The valuing of multiple forms of evidence was readily apparent in the meetings we observed. For example, as teachers considered class placements for the following year, they relied on an increasing number of forms of data. As Carla explained, "We're constantly trying to balance the groups. So instead of just looking at their Trimester 3 report cards . . . because it's a little bit subjective, we also throw into there the benchmark assessment scores" the following year. Especially when it came to placement and at report card time, teachers grappled with how to measure student learning.

Like the teachers at Chavez, these Dewey teachers considered students' progress over time and thought about the students holistically. As Ella said,

> I like that formative . . . I like to see growth over time. I like to see on here checkmarks that go all the way across, or if they start, suddenly it

clicked in right here, and now she's or he's off and running. I like to see this kind of thing. I like to see a whole big picture of how they're doing. And then, too, you know, I'm looking at, "Okay, what's going on in that child's life?" . . . I like to give them a bunch of opportunities and then I feel as though I can look at the whole big picture.

The use of whiteboard tables and iPads also gave teachers a way to capture students' learning in real time. Carla explained:

So one of the great things about these [whiteboard] tables, beyond what the students are giving to me, is that if I have to erase them . . . I can just snap a picture of it on my iPad and then we can either project it the next day and just pick up where we left off. I can print them out if needed, if I want the kids to add to it. Sometimes I will take a picture of what they brainstormed on the table and when they come the next morning, if we're moving on right away, it'll just be taped in the middle. Here's where we were yesterday, and then we continue outside of it almost like a web, so that they're adding to it.

Or if I need to change it, if the lesson wasn't going exactly in the direction that I wanted it to go, or that I see, "Oh, there's a need that I didn't know was there and I'm adapting to that," I can print it out and put it in the middle and then steer them this way or move into whatever area I discovered that they needed a little more support in. And we'll just continue on our tables, and then also to be able to flip them up when we're done and use it as a gallery.

At one meeting, teachers weighed how they could best measure students' reading comprehension. Marcia wondered out loud, "Is it okay to use writing to assess reading?" She explained that in reading students' writing she could also assess their comprehension: "But does it have to be in writing? Can't it be verbal?" she asked. "And it is teacher judgment," she said. A district staff person had visited their meeting that day and encouraged them to use a variety of measures, including a chart during discussions to note how students are articulating their learning. The team then discussed the fact that the types of questions students ask in discussions can also provide information on their level of comprehension. Marcia raised the example of a particular student who asked very good questions, but her writing was not strong, and thus she "can't judge her by her writing."

The valuing of multiple forms of evidence was also apparent in teachers' classroom practices. Teachers developed their own methods for gathering observational data on student learning to inform instructional planning. Ella used daily logs as a way to provide feedback on students' writing. She explained that she saw these "huge improvements" since she began to give them daily feedback on their work. In Marcia's classroom, as students worked in groups to solve a complex math problem, she walked around the room and took notes on a form she created. She used the form to record students' problem-solving strategies, a compliment she could later give students about their work, a teaching point for a small group, or future teaching notes for the class as a whole. This helped her more systematically document student learning in class and link her observations to both her instructional decisions and her evaluations of student progress.

Ella explained that to further chart students' progress in mathematics over the course of a term, Marcia used the following approach to document student learning in a notebook: "Each kid has a page—so it's the expectations of that trimester, those standards. And each child has a page and [Marcia] highlights when they're successful with something, and then she can look at the end where the holes were." These organically created tools helped the teachers think about student learning broadly and also specifically in relation to the state standards.

Critical Conversations About Curriculum and Pedagogy

Deep learning among teachers involves taking a critical stance on curriculum and pedagogy. At one vertical collaboration meeting we observed, the teachers debated the merits of timed tests for math fluency and turned to one of us to ask what the research said about their effectiveness. In another conversation, teachers spent quite a bit of time discussing the merits of the different writing programs they were using or piloting in their classrooms. Most of the discussion was focused on the rigor and craft of writing and what strategies might help students produce reach writing goals.

Reading was also a focal point of this team's work and of the district as a whole. The teachers taught each other strategies they had used to meet the new standards. They drew on each teacher's particular strengths and interests. Ella reflected,

> That's been kind of my strength—using authentic text and drawing kids into texts that have different reading levels. So one of our reading goals this year is that I would pick those texts and help Carla and Marcia with lessons on how different kids would access those texts.

Teachers on this team read widely and pulled teaching strategies and content from a variety of sources and then shared them with each other. As Ella explained, "We'd read a book . . . on implicit and explicit text, and I said, 'Hey, I found this page right here, and you should see the dialogue.'" She explained that her colleague replied, "I never would have seen that. . . . I could have read that book five times." She continued, "So I typed it out, and there's a whole new lesson for that." Teachers were constantly seeking new resources to share with their students, eschewing the idea of using the same ones year after year. Ella explained, "In this book I just read, I've pulled three different lessons out of it, and I've never even read the book before . . . It keeps me alive." Notably, her colleagues viewed her as an important source of knowledge on new literature to integrate into their classes.

Striving for Continuous Improvement and Embracing Innovation

Although they saw themselves as a strong team, Ella, Carla, and Marcia were also self-reflective in their need to continuously improve their practice. They looked for opportunities for feedback about their teaching and for learning new ways in which they could grow. For example, at one point Ella said she felt she had reached a plateau in her teaching: "It's kind of like, right now, I hired a personal trainer for yoga. I'm kind of at that plateau. I'm still falling over every time I do this pose. I need somebody to [tell me] . . . what am I doing wrong?" Many teachers feel as though they could use inspiration at times. For teachers who were part of this team, the boost came primarily from other members of the team.

Teachers who were part of the team at Dewey often felt they were ready to take their teaching to a higher level. Inevitably, professional development activities aimed at a range of teachers do not always focus on teachers' individual needs. Just as their principal recognized the need for differentiated support for teachers, the teachers realized that their colleagues might be at different places in their professional development. As Ella noted, "Where we're at, I need to be digging into the standards." She said, "I would like our focus to start digging into the writing again and how we can incorporate different methods." As Marcia explained, the team was eager to move ahead: "We can't slow down. I mean our job is just like the students' job. We need to continue to progress, because you're not going to hold back the students in your classroom."

Members of the team learned a lot from watching and listening to each other. As Marcia said, "I watch the way [Carla and Ella] do it, or when we all gather in one group and talk." Carla explained, "We just experiment with that, and then during our Tuesday team meetings, a lot of times one of us will come in and say, 'I found this great program and here's how I'm using it.'" Reflecting on new technology tools they had integrated in their classroom, Carla said, "Those first couple months were hard because you had to rethink everything, but then it just becomes so seamless." This experience was formative because, as this teacher explained, "The thing that it did for us is changed . . . where we felt the boundaries were."

The team embraced innovation. In the same year they also experimented with collaborative project-based learning activities that involved students from all three classrooms working together. Carla reflected, "Probably all three of the [design thinking activities] that we did this year, we could have done in a traditional classroom, but our minds weren't open to all of that." As Ella explained, "It just starts flowing and it's amazing. You know we've got three under our belt, and all were so completely different. But I think that the district wants to start using our model."

Ella explained that their most recent project started out with a team conversation about how to address a reading standard in their classes. The teachers saw an opening for deep learning on the part of the students. For example, one standard involved having students understand that novels can be adapted into movies or plays. Instead of simply showing students a movie adaptation of a novel they were reading, the teachers involved all of their students in cross-classroom groups to develop sections of script based on the novel they were reading. They involved volunteer actors from a local theater who gave workshops to students and then acted out the scenes the students had written. This was an incredibly meaningful experience for the students, who learned not only what was involved in moving from a novel to a script, but who were also exposed to the craft of acting. Students were empowered by seeing their scripts come to life with professional actors. As Carla said, "Even though it was adapted from a book they all knew, they still took such ownership. And to capture them on that creative level because a typical school day doesn't lend itself to that kind of creation, it was the highlight of their year."

Marcia reflected on the development and implementation of these whole-grade learning activities as being formative for their professional learning: "We had a different sort of dynamic where we did a lot of cross mixing, too, with the projects that we did . . . I feel like this year I was pushed a lot in good ways." Carla said, "It certainly made us tighter as a team because we were starting to plan everything together and [we were] depending on one another. And then we learned that, 'Oh my gosh, my teammates completely and totally trust what I'm doing—and I, them.' I think, looking back, it's been a really awesome year."

Just like the teachers at Chavez, the teachers on this team at Dewey used any and all time they had together. They not only willingly worked together, but they sought out every opportunity to do so. This helped them co-manage the demands of teaching, whether it was incorporating new innovations or strategizing about how to address the needs of their students.

Conclusion

What can be learned from the Dewey case about collaborating for deep learning? A principal or district administrator could read this case and decide to more loosely structure professional learning time to allow teachers the time and space to be more creative. In many schools, this would be a strong departure from the norm of tightly prescribed PLC agendas with insufficient time for deep faculty dialogue. This could be a useful strategy, but it won't go far unless it is accompanied by a set of deliberate shifts in how we think about the teaching profession. In Chapter 3, we talked about the need to cultivate genuine respect for teachers' professional knowledge, garnering coherence around the goals of schooling and beliefs about the value of evidence and providing more time for informal collaboration among teachers. These are all important aspects of collaborating toward deep learning.

Key Takeaways and Reflection Points

- **Teachers need opportunities to engage in meaningful inquiry.** In order to realize the goal of professional collaboration, teachers must be supported to engage in inquiry about what students should know and be able to do. This goes beyond an examination of data on student learning, which is typically the charge for PLCs. Leaders should ask themselves, to what extent does the charge for collaboration allow for this?
- **Teachers' observations of student learning need to be seen as a valuable source of evidence.** For example, teachers could make notes about student thinking and future teaching points based on their observations of students working together in the classroom. These observations support teachers' professional judgment and complement other forms of data on student learning.
- **Teachers need flexibility to make pedagogical decisions,** as the dialogue around these decisions can inspire them and support them to share pedagogical knowledge. It is important for leaders to consider whether policies and practices support or constrain teachers in this endeavor.
- **Teachers should be encouraged to become critical consumers of educational resources.** For leaders, this involves inviting teachers to experiment with resources that the district or school may consider adopting and inviting critiques of those resources.
- **Teacher teams need opportunities to adopt innovations and deepen their knowledge in areas that are particular passions for them.** Feeling inspired and motivated is an important part of teachers' work. Leadership can play an important role in identifying and/or supporting teams to find what moves them individually and collaboratively.

- **Leaders must value and support teacher learning.** Leaders also play an important role in supporting differentiated learning in ways that fit with their needs. At a policy level, then, it becomes necessary to consider: What supports and what inhibits teacher learning?

For deep learning to take place in the context of professional collaboration, teachers' knowledge must be genuinely valued. Teaching needs to be seen as complex work that requires ongoing inquiry in order to be continually energizing. Unfortunately, many educational policy and reform measures do not begin with these premises, as we will explain next, in Chapter 5.

Reference

Hargreaves, A., & O'Connor, M. T. (2018). *Collaborative professionalism: When teaching together means learning for all.* Thousand Oaks, CA: Corwin Press.

5
Collaborating Through Shifting Policies

As the policy landscape continually changes around schools, including policies about what counts as student progress and meaningful instructional practice, teachers grapple with not just *how* to collaborate but also with *what* to collaborate on. In such cases, professional collaboration is about learning how to stand on solid ground and about figuring out how to make teaching meaningful while dealing with rapid changes made by others. In an era of accountability and centralization with increasing numbers of standardized programs and assessments, the frustrations that teachers face are real and must be acknowledged.

In this chapter, we describe how one school, Anthony Elementary School, dealt with these challenges. In so doing, we describe efforts to engage in productive joint work when teachers feel disempowered, context is ignored, and learning opportunities are few. The Anthony case study is not an exemplar. Professional collaboration can be messy; the reality of meshing different personalities, perspectives, and goals makes it so. We share Anthony's story because it is so typical and familiar to many educators. It is a story where the desire and motivation for engaging in professionally rewarding collaboration and professional learning exist but have yet to be tapped or nurtured by leaders or systems. At Anthony, amidst shifting expectations, we observed educators:

- being thirsty for opportunities to learn;
- attempting to learn the nuts and bolts of required changes despite a lack of supports and resources; and

- desiring uninterrupted professional collaboration that met their needs.

The experiences of teachers at Anthony stand in contrast to the experiences of teachers at Dewey and Chavez, both of which had strong histories of teacher professional collaboration. Thus, we also examine the potential for moving toward meaningful professional collaboration, acknowledging the starting point of the educators in this type of system. Indeed, the evolution toward meaningful professional collaboration has to start somewhere. By revisiting Dewey and Chavez, we find that successful collaborators manage internal interactions while mitigating or buffering external demands or expectations. Striving to find value and inspiration in teachers' work is an essential core of professional collaboration. Teachers at Dewey and Chavez were able to collectively navigate shifting district and state policies in order to sustain collaboration while managing external demands and expectations. These schools experienced:

- professional collaboration time that was sustained and protected from competing external demands; and
- collective sensemaking and integration of curricular changes to their existing practices.

Before turning to the themes we witnessed in the collaborations at Anthony, Dewey, and Chavez, we first describe the shifting federal, state, and local policy context that has so significantly shaped the work of educators.

Shifting Federal, State, and Local Policies

Educational accountability policies are increasingly broadening what counts as student achievement and school success. In the United States, the Every Student Succeeds Act has expanded measures of student success beyond English language arts and math achievement results on standardized tests to include English learner proficiency, graduation rates (for high schools), and one academic and one non-academic measure chosen at the state level. As the United States transitions out of the era of No Child Left Behind and into Every Student Succeeds, some states have also adopted new standards based on the

Common Core State Standards, which brought a new standardized testing program. The Smarter Balanced Assessment Consortium was implemented in some states, requiring schools to administer an annual adaptive online test to students in grades 3–8 and in high school. Similar to other schools that are under-resourced, the teachers at Anthony Elementary School were trying to hold steady and go about the daily work of teaching and learning despite waves of changes and top-down policies hitting them from the federal, state, and district levels.

A Glimpse Into Anthony Elementary

Anthony is situated in a small urban district that was experiencing major leadership turnover the year we began our study. The turnover, typical for urban districts, was not new to Anthony, as it had undergone a revolving door of superintendents and other district administrators for several years. With the hiring of a new superintendent, the district office underwent restructuring and the implementation of new program initiatives. Thus, in addition to managing the federal and state accountability changes, Anthony was navigating district changes at the same time.

Nested in a densely populated neighborhood surrounded by apartment complexes, single-family homes, and businesses, Anthony Elementary is easy to overlook. The cozy school building and its staff serve students who are predominantly from Latinx backgrounds, with more than 90 percent qualifying for the free- and reduced-price lunch program, and 60 percent designated as English Language learners. A small office building houses the principal's office and staff lounge; it bustles with energy as parents, students, and teachers stream in and out throughout the day. Walls dotted with student artwork welcome visitors with colorful displays. The arts program was an initiative that the principal had enthusiastically supported. The atmosphere of the school is calm and unassuming. Anthony feels and looks like a typical school and, in many respects, it is.

For over five years, the principal at Anthony was a source of steady leadership. She was very familiar with the district, as she started there as a teacher before becoming an administrator. Faculty described the principal as someone who was knowledgeable about teaching and student support. As the only full-time administrator on campus, she was a visible presence throughout the school day and knew all of the school's 500 students by name. Throughout the year, she was expected to communicate to her staff and parents the major changes and mandates instituted by the district, with some of the decisions arriving with less than two weeks' notice. There was quite a bit of uncertainty as the new district administration restructured and developed new strategic plans. Thus, quite a large portion of the principal's time was spent on communicating change efforts and attempting to justify reasons for changes when she had not been in on the decision-making herself.

As the principal tried to mediate district mandates and changes, teachers at Anthony responded in various ways. The team of teachers that spanned two grade levels was composed of veteran teachers who had been working at Anthony for five to more than 10 years. Some of these teachers were trying to "roll with the punches" by keeping a focus on their own classroom and teams, while others were frustrated or disengaged. Simultaneously, there was a consistent hunger for learning opportunities and support to do their work more effectively.

Thirsty for Opportunities to Learn

With new reform and policy mandates, teachers respond in a variety of ways—from accommodation and assimilation to outright resistance (Coburn, 2004; Cuban, 2013; Datnow, Hubbard, & Mehan, 2002). From a policy perspective or leaders' viewpoint, teacher resistance is often viewed as a problem or hurdle for implementation. As a reaction to reform with little time to build capacity or understand what new knowledge and practices teachers are being asked to take on, however, resistance to new mandates is logical. Teacher resistance can make "good sense" (Gitlin & Margonis, 1995). As both the objects of reform and the front-line change agents, teachers have to figure out the technical aspects of implementing new standards, programs, and curricula while also acquiring new knowledge and skills themselves—all under public and administrative scrutiny to produce student achievement results (Cuban, 2013).

Rather than resistance to change, educators at Anthony expressed frustration about not having the opportunity to learn. They expressed a thirst for professional learning opportunities that would enable them to increase their effectiveness and help them to understand what was being asked of them. In short, they were parched for knowledge. One teacher, Melissa, explained this frustration with respect to the new computer program initiative:

> So we're all thirsty for this. For me, personally, I need to get my technology up to speed. And I know that that way I can better serve all the students if I was a little bit more tech savvy. They [district administrators] need to offer more really good quality staff development.

The teachers' desire for learning opportunities was not simply a reflection of their goal to increase their effectiveness. Teachers like Melissa also expressed a sense of moral obligation. That is, if the district and public were going to invest in new standards, new technology, and new programs, then teachers needed to know how to use it effectively.

Changes to curriculum, standards, and assessments, in addition to new intervention programs with new technological requirements and skills, made teachers feel as though new expectations were being "thrown" at them. As another teacher, Shannon, shared:

> Figuring out these new things that they're just throwing at me from the district office and how am I going to fit something new into my day? You know we have [a new computerized reading and math intervention program], and then you have the whole new getting them ready for the new testing on the computer. How do I know what's important, where's the balance, what do I keep, what do I get rid of?

Too often, change is mandated from the state or from the district without consideration of what it would take for teachers to implement the new expectations effectively (Cuban, 2013). Consideration of how these various reform efforts complement one another is also often missing. Teachers are left to figure out how to make new mandates work for their day-to-day practice and for the benefit of their students. Shannon's quote also reflects a thoughtful response in weighing all the changes. She asks critical questions: *What are valuable uses of teachers' time? What do they keep and what do they let go of, given time and resource constraints?*

Due to lack of time, resources, or planning, Anthony's teachers rarely received ongoing or sustained professional development. Both the principal and the teachers acknowledged that part of the problem was the lack of substitute teacher coverage. In order for teachers to attend professional development trainings for major programs and curricula that were held during school hours, they needed someone to cover their classes and lessons. The district as a whole was struggling with finding substitute teachers—a problem that other neighborhood districts were also experiencing.

At the same time, as some of the teachers acknowledged, there were no established processes or structures for productive collaborations that were teacher-led and that focused on instructional needs beyond changes mandated by the administration. During weekly staff meetings held after school for an hour, the principal would set the agenda. The meetings would often start with news and updates. Then, ideally, the bulk of the time would be devoted to grade-level team meetings. Throughout the first year of the study, however, this rarely occurred. Instead, much of the meeting time was taken over with news and updates from the districts and the technical realities of implementing new curricula, assessment procedures, and programs.

For example, mid-fall, a new reading intervention program was adopted by the district and expected to be implemented in that same month. The program was intended to support differentiated instruction through adaptive diagnostic testing and activities tailored to individual student levels in English language arts. All students were expected to take the diagnostic and benchmark assessments, and schools were given schedules for testing periods. Training was done through a trickle-down approach: The principal and/or key support staff on leadership teams would get the formal training and then go back to their school sites to conduct schoolwide training. When asked about all the changes, Melissa talked about the negative impact:

> You know, we've had so many superintendents. So it's just, honestly, the ones who suffer the most are the kids . . . Not me. I mean, I'll roll with the punches, whatever, but it's too many people changing the stuff in the middle of the game.

Toward the end of the first semester, the principal announced at a faculty meeting that teachers would have additional collaboration time. She talked about the collaboration schedule and expressed hope that it would lead to more "successful time and more time to collaborate with peers." About half the teachers murmured that this would be great. However, one teacher asked, "Is that up to us, the agenda? Or is it someone else's?" The principal didn't give a direct yes or no answer but mentioned that they would basically have to work within the district's focus on improving writing and English language development. Alas, the collaboration time was only about 30 minutes once a week for each grade-level team, which left little time for anything substantive to occur in these meetings.

Learning the Nuts and Bolts

As mentioned earlier, rather than being resistant to change, teachers at Anthony wanted opportunities to learn more about how new programs and expectations would support their instruction and student learning. They wanted opportunities to make sense of these reforms in light of their existing practices and skill sets. Research on policy implementation notes that educators sometimes take up reform in superficial ways and misread policy intentions to fit with their pre-existing experiences and knowledge. Thus, the cognitive aspects of learning new practices must be considered (Spillane, Reiser, & Reimer, 2002). Before they can become experts, educators need opportunities to learn the "nuts and bolts" of a practice or program.

Below we share a vignette of a team meeting that describes Anthony teachers reviewing a new computer intervention program. They discussed how to differentiate instruction using this new program, focusing on the logistics of accessing the lessons available and how to allocate time to students, given the mandated time requirements for program use. This vignette reflects the teachers' desire to learn as well as their need to understand the logistics and technical aspects of implementation before they feel comfortable with experimenting and figuring out what aspects of a program they want to keep or let go.

> *After 20 minutes of news and announcements, the principal allowed grade-level teams to disperse into separate groups. In one group, six teachers joined together for a conversation. The group began to talk about the computer-based intervention program implementation, and Shannon offered to show the*

lessons available on the program, moving to the front of the class to use the projector.

Shannon logged in as a student to show an available lesson on comprehension and phonics. As they reviewed it, Melissa commented, "This is extensive for something they just threw at us." Shannon concurred, stating, "They should've trained teachers on it first." As Shannon worked to get the lesson playing, at one point the screen froze. Erica commented, "That's what it does. It freezes on us." Luis added a comment about lessons repeating. Several teachers replied that didn't happen to them, but logging on could be problematic.

Melissa commented about the time, mentioning that 1.5 to 2 hours per student each week seems like a lot. Erica replied that it would be about 25 minutes per student each day. They began to talk about their existing English language arts curriculum and what they used. Erica asked Shannon about her plan for grouping students and how she did small group instruction. Shannon replied, "Since there are five days in a week, I'll probably meet with Profile 1 a couple of times a week—at least—and less with Profile 5. And with Profile 1, it looks like I have about nine to 10 students, so I may have to split them in two groups." Melissa asked, "Do you do pre-teaching? Or how do you do it?" Shannon stated that she doesn't really do pre-teaching and pulls up a sample lesson from the program to show that it isn't necessary, and that she just "works [her] way through the lesson." Erica asked, "Do you have timelines for yourself, or see how it goes? For example, do you just do the groups 15 to 20 minutes?" Shannon replied that she usually spends 15 to 30 minutes for the groups/lessons. Erica then queried, "How did you know how long the lessons went? Did you time yourself?" At this point, they went back and forth about managing the different groups, and other teachers also chimed in.

The questions raised by teachers at this juncture of implementation and collaboration were a reflection of their attempts to make sense of the technical and pedagogical aspects of using a new program. Rather than simple resistance, they were trying to figure out what the program could contribute to their instructional practice. They were also trying to make sense of balancing the mandated requirements of the program usage set forth by the district with their existing instructional approaches. This was all necessary, as none of the teachers had been given formal training or an introduction to the program. Their existing knowledge was self-taught and acquired without any expert support.

Thus, they used their collaboration time to learn the nuts and bolts with one another.

Collaboration Interrupted

Despite Anthony's efforts to develop ongoing professional collaboration time focused on teachers' problems of practice and instructional planning, too often meetings covered a multitude of topics. The following vignette illustrates how 45 minutes of collaboration time was typically filled:

> *During one team meeting, Melissa and Erica started by deciding to just focus on their common planning for writing. Melissa asked about how the novel study was going, and Erica listed out everything that was going well; "They love inside/outside circle." She added that it was great that students were hearing so many different voices and perspectives and that they got to share their writing with one another. She thought that her students had greatly improved in their writing and said she had been really pushing them to expand and elaborate their writing.*
>
> *They continued to share about the improvement they've seen in their students' writing. Melissa noted, "There's been a huge change." Erica replied, "Especially with weekly writing and writing with details." Erica then shared about the Cesar Chavez writing and poster assignment required by the district. She mentioned that she was having students pull Cesar Chavez quotes and asked them, "How can you relate it to your lives?" She also told them, "Every day you write. You're all authors." She went on to share with a big smile that, "It was cute to see their faces when I mentioned that they were all authors."*
>
> *At this point, the principal entered the room and announced that she would like to share some information about the state testing procedures. She recently went to a district meeting and suggested that they will have to help their kids build testing stamina. She also shared some test preparation resources with them. The principal and teachers continued to talk about the high-stakes nature of these tests and the increased expectations that come with it. They wrapped up their conversation and the principal left.*
>
> *After the principal's departure, Melissa asked how much time they had left. They noted that they had less than 10 minutes and jumped right into the planning they needed to cover, including the daily writing topics and field trip*

planning. Melissa opened up her planning calendar and Erica pulled out the writing prompt cards. Erica read out some of the prompts, and they decided which ones they would use on which day.

This collaboration time, originally intended to focus on developing writing lessons, was interrupted by preparation and requirements for the new testing process. As much as the principal wanted to provide and protect teacher collaboration, she also had to take time to inform teachers of new requirements and expectations that they would need to consider for their planning.

In general, teachers at Anthony wanted collaboration time with one another, on the condition that it would be productive. When asked about the benefits of collaboration, one teacher shared, "I like it a lot because you get to learn new strategies from each other. It just was an eye opener rather than just focusing on your own lessons. I guess by hearing them you get to be more creative, yeah." Similarly, a second teacher shared,

> When we get together and plan, as we did this year, it is very useful. But in the past . . . if you have two people that kind of have a bad attitude about faculty meetings and three people that want it to be productive, then that's not so productive. Then that's when personality plays into it.

A third teacher acknowledged that alone time in the classroom would be preferable to attending the grade-level team meetings, although once in a while it was useful: "I prefer to stay in the classroom, to be honest with you, sometimes. I mean, come on. It's always good to meet and sit down and talk about what we are doing, actually. It's good because, other than that, we don't have the time."

Shannon noted that collaboration had been more productive than in the past because there was a schoolwide focus on writing: "I think this year they were better than they had been in the past because we were more focused on writing as a whole staff. I think in the past we'd have grade-level meetings that just weren't as focused." She attributed part of the success to the fact that staff developed the goals themselves rather than them being mandated from the district:

> At a staff meeting everyone had decided that's what we wanted to focus on. So then we went to our leadership team meetings and made our

goals for the year. Then we were able to share that with the staff, and they all were on board. But I think if we would have just said we're focusing on writing this year, without having any of their input, it wouldn't have gone as well as it did.

Holding Steady at Dewey

The case of Anthony illuminates the struggles that teachers face as they attempt to navigate shifting external demands within a structure and culture that do not consistently support professional collaboration and teacher learning. This contrasts with Dewey, where, as we explained in Chapter 4, teachers engaged in ongoing and sustained professional learning opportunities guided by relevant problems of practice. Even at Dewey, however, teachers had to find ways to sustain this work in the face of competing demands that are an inevitable part of teachers' professional lives.

As we explained in Chapter 4, in the first year of our study at Dewey, teachers experienced a great deal of autonomy to set goals for collaborative work and plan activities accordingly. The following year, however, a new district initiative for professional development occupied quite a bit of teachers' collaborative time, marking a significant shift from the prior year when teachers had much more control over their time. The shift in collaborative time was fueled by a positive intent on the part of the district, where administrators decided to use some early release days to bring teachers together across and within schools to engage in professional development activities. They quickly learned how precious this collaborative time was for teachers.

Teachers missed the time with their immediate team colleagues, and this led to concern among teachers. One teacher, Jessica, explained: "This year, all that time is pulling us apart . . . That's been kind of frustrating." Some teachers questioned whether the cross-school professional development was the best use of their time, as they did not feel it responded to needs in their classroom contexts. As one teacher said, "It wasn't specific to where we are." Jessica remarked that the professional development sessions were "just more getting information and not necessarily looking at student work and planning of our work. I think that's been impacting us, feeling as though we're stressed out too."

Teachers voiced a strong preference for more flexible yet goal-oriented time: "I really liked last year how we had the time... I mean, if you give us a topic and just let us do it, I'm okay with that. You know, even if you say at the end of January we need this, this, and this from you, but you get the time to do it," said Marcia. Ruby, another teacher at Dewey, added:

> I felt like last year our PLCs were more aligned with team time. I remember talking about that continuous cycle of learning with PLC and having set goals and coming back and making common assessments. And I haven't felt that we've been able to do much of that at all this year.

Teachers provided feedback to the principal, noting that they needed more time together. She was responsive to their needs, validated their concerns, and relayed their feedback to the district. At the same time, she also recognized the need to support district priorities. Teachers realized that it was a difficult balance, and they appreciated the support. Referring to school and district administration, Victoria said, "I think they're really good at hearing what the teachers need and making adjustments, but at the same time staying true to what they want us to get accomplished." Ruby summed up the experience by explaining that the professional development "was very purposefully planned and it was really important work that we were doing. I think it could have been maybe balanced out a little bit better with every other [PLC], or at least just knowing that we would have three really solid PLCs that didn't get interrupted that was just team time."

Teachers recognized that some professional development activities and cross-school collaboration opportunities were useful. A teacher at Dewey acknowledged, "I think the district in general does a good job of getting people together." But teachers also felt there was sometimes a lack of time to fully take advantage of joint learning opportunities, as the reflective time occasionally was cut short. Because the teams we studied at Dewey worked so well together, teachers also found more value in the sustained collaborative work they were able to accomplish within their teams. One teacher noted that whereas the team was characterized by trust and openness, these same features were not always present in cross-school meetings where teachers didn't always feel comfortable sharing ideas with each other.

When teachers at Dewey joined together to share concerns about the shift in how their PLC time was allocated, they were successful in gaining back some more of their collaborative time. Unlike at Anthony, the district and school administrations were stable; they were responsive when teachers raised concerns, and they made adjustments accordingly. While this shift was being addressed, instead of abandoning their collaborative goals, teachers found ways to accomplish them within a compressed time frame. As one teacher reflected, "I think the highlight of this year was the team having to pull together to face some of the challenges that were presented to us, because you do pull together as a group to face challenges." She added, "That's all learning as well." This is a good example of how shifting expectations from the district were navigated and negotiated between teachers, the principal, and the district in a way that was productive. Teacher voices were heard and acted upon.

Navigating Curricular Shifts Collectively at Chavez

During the period of our study, all four schools were beginning to implement the Common Core State Standards, which emphasize more authentic learning opportunities for students, critical thinking, and depth of content over breadth. Dewey was probably farthest along in the uptake of these standards, in large part because they cohered with the direction the district had already been moving prior to their implementation. As explained in Chapter 3, teachers at Chavez were very clear in their expectations for student learning, and they had measurable goals for student achievement that now needed to be aligned to the Common Core standards.

The district in which Chavez was located used a phase-in approach to the Common Core standards, however, asking teachers to first implement shifts in language arts instruction and then move into math. Kayla, a teacher at Chavez, explained:

> So with Common Core they're trying to roll out a different content area each year. And so the past two years it was writing, so they started

Common Core writing, and they had trainings on that. They did professional growth days on writing, and a lot of collaborating on what writing is going to look like. And so last year is when they began math, and it was more what they call "being aware." "So this is what math looks like, here's how it looks, here's how it's going to look. Don't really do it yet in your classroom, but here's how it's going to look in the future." And then this year it's . . . we're implementing it, and so it's, "Okay, so here's Common Core math, and go."

The district's phase-in approach did not always fit with the collective mindset of the Chavez team, who saw themselves as always moving ahead. Pat explained, "So we're already trying to get ahead of the game so that we're a little more comfortable." This approach distinguished them from others in the district, but they were quick to note that collaborating with colleagues who were at different stages was always useful. As Hannah noted:

> Not to toot our own horn, but when we go to some of those [professional development activities] we kind of already are at that step, so we're kind of ready for the next step, if that makes any sense. But we always learned every time from other teachers: "What are you doing? What works well? What's not working well? How are you modifying this?" So, that was helpful.

As changes to each curricular area were phased in, professional development was provided from the district. Unlike Dewey's district, where most professional development activities involved all teachers in a school, Chavez's district was much larger and more often used a trainer-of-trainer or lead teacher model, where select teachers attended trainings at the district and brought back their learnings to share with colleagues. The intention was that there would be teachers at every site who could serve as resources.

Across the schools, teachers didn't always feel fully prepared for the shift to the Common Core Standards. Some teachers found it challenging to implement the new standards in their classrooms and wished for more guidance, particularly with the sequencing of the standards. One teacher wondered whether the curricular materials accompanying the new standards would best support students' learning, stating: "The curriculum, we feel, isn't what's best for kids." The shift in standards conflicted with some teachers' belief systems about how best to teach or what to teach. These are common sentiments that are often brought about by reform.

Chavez also differed from Dewey in that, before Common Core implementation, teaching practices tended to be slightly more traditional rather than constructivist. During the years of our study, teachers at Dewey did not have a math text to rely upon, as the expectation was that they would draw from a variety of more updated sources. Chavez, on the other hand, had a district-adopted math text that was intended to be supplemented as needed. However, some teachers found that the math resources and learning expectations of Common Core were not a natural fit and did not cohere with what they felt students could do. Kayla explained how this played out at Chavez:

> Half [of the students] are English learners. . . . When it's all reading and word problems, it's overwhelming, and they're not teaching them just the standard algorithms anymore. It's, nope, just word problems and read, read, read. And even if they can do standard multiplication, seeing it in words and. . . So this year it's math, and we're just figuring out as we go.

This statement reveals that teachers at Chavez struggled to reconcile the new math standards with how they thought about their students' instructional needs. Although teachers were interested in experimenting with innovative ways of teaching math, they felt that their curricular materials did not offer an easy bridge between the more traditional algorithms students were accustomed to and the new, more authentic problem-solving expectations of the Common Core standards.

While they differed in some ways, Chavez and Dewey were very similar in their strong cultures of teacher professional collaboration. This strong culture and structure proved to be tremendously useful at Chavez as teachers collectively managed implementation of the Common Core standards in their classrooms. As Chavez teacher Courtney explained, "There was a lot of discussion, every unit, of, what should be our emphasis? How are we going make the assessment worthwhile so that it gives us information, gives the kids information, and assesses actually what and how we are teaching?"

This was a particular challenge, as the teachers did not feel that the embedded assessments were reliable. As one teacher said:

> I think that was a big obstacle for us. . . They're presenting things on the assessment nowhere near how it was presented in the pages of the book,

nor in the way we presented it as teachers. So that was a huge obstacle for us, every unit. And I think from . . . in listening to other people's discussion, I think they felt the same way in [other grades].

Teachers found that they needed to spend a lot of time dialoguing first about how to understand the standards, then about how their materials supported them (or didn't), and then about how to assess students on the new standards.

District and site leadership recognized the need for Chavez teachers to learn to implement the new standards together and allocated entire days for teams to collaborate. The teachers explained how they puzzled through new standards together in these dedicated days, which they found invaluable. Hannah described how this played out surrounding the reading curriculum:

> The first one we focused on reading because that one was early in the year. And we looked at the new Common Core standards and we figured out, "Okay, we're going to teach this skill in this trimester, we're going to teach this skill in this trimester, this skill in this trimester." So that was kind of an all-day thing. The second time we focused on writing, and then . . . we went to another school site with other fifth grade teachers and did math.

And likewise, Rachel described their discussion about writing:

> Our Common Core days . . . a lot of it was dedicated also last year to writing . . . just trying to figure out the whole idea of the opinion piece coming in and what that meant, and what . . . opinion versus persuasive. And what kind of shifts, you know, were happening there.

The district could only support these full-day planning sessions for one year, but nonetheless, they were critical in allowing the teachers time to wrap their minds around the new standards and how they would shape their practice. Teams were given the flexibility to decide when to schedule these days. As Pat explained,

> I know every grade-level team on our site had three release days . . . Some used them over summer, some are using them during the school year. But just they're Common Core days to just sit down as a team and figure out what's happening here, what's the transition.

Although the teachers at Chavez initially faced some challenges integrating the new curricular standards into their practice, the structure of collaboration support provided by the district and school leadership made the shift much more manageable. In this respect, the circumstances at Chavez were quite different from those at Anthony, where consistent time for collaboration was hard to come by. The teachers at Chavez had also developed a strong culture for collaboration long before the implementation of the Common Core State Standards, which allowed them to move relatively smoothly through the transition. This buffered them in much the same way that teachers at Dewey experienced. For these reasons, regular collaboration time that could be flexibly used by teachers was invaluable.

Conclusion

Protecting and preserving professional collaboration doesn't just mean allowing the space and time for it to occur, although that is indeed essential. It also means recognizing that these collaborative spaces are the means by which teachers filter and make sense of educational policy shifts (Coburn, 2001; Spillane et al., 2002). The three contrasting cases in this chapter make this abundantly clear. These cases bring to light the various ways in which district professional development and teacher professional collaboration intersect. In general, teachers across the schools did not find that planned opportunities for professional learning, unless it was collaboration time, were particularly helpful in addressing their immediate needs. Yet collaboration time cannot be the only avenue for teacher learning, as sometimes there are challenges related to expertise, social dynamics, or motivation.

In these three cases, we also see some interesting patterns in terms of the implied level of trust between administrators and teachers, as well as in the level of power that teachers hold. At both Dewey and Chavez, teachers had earned a certain amount of respect through their collective work, and thus their voices were eventually heard and trusted when it came to decision-making about shifting policies. Although challenges inevitably arose in the process of shifting policies, but both schools existed in districts that operated under an assumption of teacher professionalism and expertise. At Anthony, on the other hand, a revolving door of leaders and a top-down structure and culture of decision-making made it difficult for teachers to have a voice. In all cases, it is clear that in order to understand how professional collaboration is built and sustained, the four Ps—people, practices, policies, and patterns—need to be examined. Supporting the development of deep and purposeful professional collaboration will require leaders to think through all of these elements.

Key Takeaways and Reflection Points

- **Professional collaboration can help teachers move through policy changes.** Given the important role of collaboration as a buffer in the change process, consideration needs to be given to how it can be protected and preserved. Leaders often have to make difficult decisions about whether to preserve high-functioning teams as a group whose members sustain each other professionally, or whether to spread the wealth by dispersing those teachers to other teams that may be functioning less well together, with the aim of overall school improvement.
- **Leaders must protect the integrity of professional collaboration time for teachers.** Valuable collaboration time is often occupied with competing agendas. Collaboration time is often insufficient to produce the kind of deep learning that is embedded in professional development expectations. Even leaders who espouse to protect teachers' time struggle with this issue. Leaders would be wise to ask themselves, to what degree do accountability demands—or administrative agendas more generally—occupy valuable professional collaboration time for teachers? How can professional development be planned in ways that capitalize on and support, rather than detract from, teachers' collective professionalism? What new models may need to be entertained in order for this to occur?
- **Leaders must create and sustain a culture that reflects the value and importance of teachers' professional wisdom.** This is important in all aspects of school and district functioning. Often leaders will convey respect for teachers but then approach policy implementation in a top-down fashion or adopt scripted

curricula that make teachers feel as though their knowledge isn't recognized. Leaders would be wise to reflect on the ways that policy implementation strategies and daily practices communicate to teachers that their professional wisdom is valued.

References

Coburn, C. E. (2001). Collective sense-making about reading: How teachers mediate reading policy in their professional communities. *Educational Evaluation and Policy Analysis, 23*(2), 145–170.

Coburn, C. E. (2004). Beyond decoupling: Rethinking the relationship between the institutional environment and the classroom. *Sociology of Education, 77*(3), 211–244.

Cuban, L. (2013). Why so many structural changes in schools and so little reform in teaching practice? *Journal of Educational Administration, 51*(2), 109–125.

Datnow, A., Hubbard, L., & Mehan, H. (2002). *Extending educational reform: From one school to many.* London: Routledge Falmer.

Gitlin, A., & Margonis, F. (1995). The political aspect of reform: Teacher resistance as good sense. *American Journal of Education, 103*(4), 377–405.

Spillane, J. P., Reiser, B. J., & Reimer, T. (2002). Policy implementation and cognition: Reframing and refocusing implementation research. *Review of Educational Research, 72*(3), 387–431.

6

Collaborating With Emotion

We have touched upon the topic of emotions in other chapters. Many of the examples we have provided thus far exemplify the positive emotions associated with collaboration. In these instances, teachers have not only willingly worked together, but they have sought out opportunities to do so. Their experience contrasts sharply with the experience of many other teachers who feel (and often are) forced to work together and do not find benefit in collaborating with their colleagues. Whereas time flew when teachers in the former category worked together, teachers in many other team meetings cannot wait for the meetings to end. Thus, perceptions of collaborative time vary a great deal depending on the value and emotions that teachers associate with it.

In Chapter 2, we talked about mindsets for professional collaboration that is driven by a deep moral commitment to equity and excellence for all students. In Chapters 3 and 4, the joy that teachers experienced working with each other was clear. In Chapter 5, we described the frustration and stress that teachers feel when new initiatives require professional collaboration and threaten it at the same time. In this chapter we delve more deeply into this range of emotions and talk about what professional collaboration can do to support teachers emotionally. We also explore the role of teachers' emotions in supporting productive professional collaboration.

Many reform efforts are put forth without attention to the emotional ups and downs that teachers experience in the process of change. The focus is often on how to get teachers to be on board with innovations without much regard for what that means emotionally, or what emotions are involved in resisting change. Although there has been increasing attention to emotions in educational change research, numerous authors have argued that emotions in this context remain understudied (Saunders, 2003; Zembylas, 2010).

Emotional Repertoires

Teaching in a climate of change can provoke feelings of inspiration, excitement, and positive energy. It can also bring fear, anxiety, and frustration. Teachers may feel ambivalent about the landscape shifting around them and also about their contradictory emotions. To some extent, this depends on whether they feel powerful or powerless in the face of the changes that are occurring (Schmidt & Datnow, 2005). We often fail to consider the "underlying emotional repertoire required by teachers if they are to sustain high quality, enthusiastic teaching on a daily basis over a career" (Day & Leitch, 2001, p. 407).

Although emotions are often considered to be an individual activity, it is important to understand how teachers emote collectively as we consider how they build their professional capital. Also, it is not just teachers' initial emotional responses to reform that matter, but also what their emotions ultimately mean for their professional engagement: "Discussions of emotionality in teachers' work form a counter-discourse to the technical-rationalist emphasis on teacher standards. While standards seek to define and prescribe the professional role that teachers play, teachers' identities are complex and socially situated within lived experiences" (O'Connor, 2008, pp. 125–126).

Even in its best form, we can't expect collaboration to fully take care of teachers' emotional needs and also be a place for planning, examination of evidence on student learning, and deep inquiry. This would be a tall order; professional collaboration can support teachers emotionally, but it can't be the only answer. On the one hand, strong communities can buffer members from external demands or resist what they consider as unnecessary or unproductive professional demands; on the other hand, these can also close off the group and keep them isolated. Teachers who are inspired and joyful about their collaboration often accomplish amazing work together, but they end up giving up a lot of their own personal time. Although we commend them, this pattern is not sustainable systemically and is unfair to teachers. A lack of time and training can bring up anxiety and stress for teachers who feel a deep sense of responsibility to provide high-quality teaching in the context of unrealistic time expectations. Obviously there needs to be more time in the professional day to enable deep learning and skill development.

It is important to know how emotions shape teacher collaboration and how teacher collaboration shapes emotion—this is an iterative process. In this chapter, we discuss the various ways in which professional collaboration can support teachers emotionally by:

- buffering them from external demands and the stress of reform and developing their collective resiliency;
- being a source of inspiration for improving practice;
- lightening the "burden" around curriculum design and instructional planning; and
- being a site for celebrating student learning.

We also discuss the emotional work of professional collaboration, which is essential to investigate as well. In particular:

- Collaboration can be draining on teachers' time and energy, especially when teachers feel the stress of not having enough time to work together.
- Professional collaboration requires interpersonal skills to deal with managing one's own emotions and those of others.
- Tight collaborative groups of teachers risk being isolated from the school and the system. This can lead to groupthink and reinforce norms of contrived collegiality, rather than promoting professional collaboration for deep learning.

We discuss each of these topics in detail in the following sections. First, we investigate the positive emotions associations with professional collaboration.

The Positive Emotions of Professional Collaboration

Buffering Teachers From the Stress of Change and Developing Collective Resiliency

As the three cases discussed in Chapter 5 made clear, the introduction of new initiatives often leads to stress for teachers. Stress related to educational reform is ubiquitous for them. Almost every teacher we spoke with described the emotional toll of adjusting to new standards, implementing new curricula, or digesting new policy demands from the district level. This was true for teachers at every career stage—new, mid-career, and experienced—and in schools ranging from urban to suburban and those in smaller and larger districts.

In one case, teachers shared frustration that stemmed from the continual churn of reforms that took away from more substantive joint work among them. As one teacher said, "They roll something out to us, we spend all this time trying to understand it, and we never talked about it again... So the powerful work never gets done." Teachers sometimes expressed emotions around the lack of trust they felt in district decision-making: "There was some transparency. There's not any anymore."

Similar to the teachers in a study by Zembylas and Barker (2007), teachers in the four schools we studied filtered—and, in some cases, managed—the stress associated with reform within their collaborative teams. Teachers in our study saw reforms originating at the district or state level as an inevitable part of their professional lives, and they developed strategies for responding to them in ways that lessened the stress involved. This response suggests a level of collective empowerment that is important.

At Billings, professional collaboration helped some teachers prioritize improving their craft rather than becoming bogged down in competing priorities. Data played a key role in helping focus their discussion. When asked to reflect on the PLC meetings, Ben shared:

> I think PLCs are just good teaching. And I think good teaching means assessing, analyzing, revisiting, and assessing again. [PLCs] make you make the time for it, but I also think they're designed to have the collaboration. What I like about the PLCs is they really, I mean just as our PLC did, it says "this is your focus and everything else, save it for later."

So, I think their beauty is this time just to discuss your PLC goal and what we're going to do about it.

Teachers reminded themselves not to become preoccupied with the shifting landscape and developed collective coping strategies for doing so. One strategy was to maintain a focus on students rather than on adult issues. As one teacher explained, "It's all about the kids, so then it did make me steer that way a little more and just kind of divert my energy in a different way. So that's a good thing." The supportive team she was a part of made all the difference. She added, "I'm just always grateful we work well together, because . . . I can see how people get really bitter."

When PLC time at Dewey was constrained due to competing demands, teachers' strong relationships with each other persisted and served as an emotional buffer. Jessica explained, "It's been making it a challenge, but then at the same time it's been okay, because I think we have a strong team where everybody's pulling their weight." Teachers knew they could rely upon one another to engage in joint work informally as well as formally.

Implementing the Common Core standards at Dewey relied heavily on teacher engagement and the co-creation of curricula, as the district had moved away from the use of textbooks. Although this was initially stressful for teachers, they emerged feeling accomplished. Victoria explained, "You know, I think it's been a really big growth year for us in general. And so I just . . . I feel like we've learned so much as a team about what we value in the curriculum and standards and how to approach it." Being part of a strong team helped support the teachers emotionally through this shift. Ruby added:

> Our team went through a lot of changes this year, but that went really well. I think we couldn't ask for a better shake out for how everything wound up with the team dynamic. I think we all complemented each other really nicely. So the year started off challenging because we just thought we had it all down, and then we had to come back to the drawing board. But we figured it out and it worked well.

As these examples suggest, strong professional communities can emotionally buffer teachers from the stress of external demands and difficult shifts that are an inevitable part of teachers' work lives.

Persevering together helped the teachers develop collective and individual resiliency in the face of change. While this had obvious positives for the teams at Dewey, tight teacher communities also have the potential to lead to isolation for other teams, as we will explain later.

Professional Collaboration as a Source of Inspiration

Teachers can derive great joy and inspiration from professional collaboration. The teachers at the schools we studied described a certain warmth from being part of a supportive team. Positive emotions were activated in the course of their learning from each other and in knowing that they could bring their problems of practice to a supportive group and come out with some new ideas. At Dewey, for example, there were many lessons about the positive emotions that teachers experienced in the course of joint work. Ruby explained in very positive terms the culture of professional collaboration at her school:

> I think from the moment that this school was created, PLC was at the forefront. And it was, "This is what we do. These are the norms of our school. We work together." Every year we would set norms for our team about respectful listening, honoring each other's time, and that we would commit to certain blocks . . . We would take pictures at the beginning of every year with our team, it would be part of our staff development. Before school started we would set our goals for the year about how we would work together as a team and what our team goal was for academic success or even social and emotional success in our classrooms and on our team.

She explained that "this really beautiful culture" was established by a prior school principal and has carried forward.

Teachers at Dewey often reflected on how invigorating it was to regularly learn from each other. For example, Ella commented, "I don't know if it's luck or just that our dynamics are such, but I'm truly amazed. Carla came in the other day and she said, 'Oh, I did a lesson on sea change,' and I asked, 'What's sea change? I have never done it that way.' And so I'm still really learning." In fact, all members of this teacher team experienced inspiration. Teachers on this gave us numerous examples of how they regularly learned from each other.

Ruby was part of a different team of teachers at Dewey. She spoke very poignantly about the importance of professional collaboration as a place to process the challenging emotions that come along with teaching and with new learning standards, and how their work together was an opportunity for pushing forward collectively for renewal:

> Of course it's not as if there aren't things that [are] challenging. . . . I think as a teacher there are plenty of times you just feel a failure, that just didn't go well or [students] did not respond well to that. I set up this great activity, and they just weren't understanding what I needed them to do. I mean all that stuff still happens all the time. But I think I've never felt so positive about the work we're doing and across the subject areas. And I think that's a direct reflection of the shift in the standards, just understanding that shift better, understanding what the expectation is for kids, having a team that's not afraid collectively that we can sit down and dig apart and say, "I don't know the answer. Let's figure it out."

Ruby added, "I think that those conversations that we have, they give me the courage to be a better teacher." The strength that she derived from this experience in professional collaboration was incredibly important. She also reflected, "I love that we have that safety on our team that we're the first people to say, 'I don't have any idea. What do you think?' I think that makes us better teachers for our kids." What if all teacher teams could provide safety for their members and also give them the courage to be stronger teachers?

Professional Collaboration Lightens Feelings of "Burden"

Professional collaboration can lessen the burdensome feelings teachers often have related to designing new curricula or engaging in instructional planning. Sharing the work can provide a sense of relief, not necessarily because it takes less time when work is done collectively, but because of teachers' positive regard for what they are able to produce together. This can also enhance teachers' feelings of confidence about the lessons they plan for their students.

At Chavez, teachers often talked about the positive emotions associated with co-planning. Hannah explained:

> The support of the team was very helpful, I mean, just being able to go over and talk with Kim and say, "I don't know what I'm doing here," or, "This seemed to be really easy for my kids," or, "This seemed to be really hard for my kids," or, "What lessons are you skipping? What lessons are you modifying?" So that collaboration piece was huge.

As we explained in Chapter 3, co-planning at Chavez was often a daily activity, often occurring outside of formal collaboration time. Kayla explained: "I'll either email the other teacher and ask, 'Hey, can I meet with you? I'm just struggling on how to teach this division strategy to these kids.' . . . But as a schedule? No. It's more, 'Hey, can we meet? Let's go over this.'"

At both Chavez and Dewey, math was an area in which teachers felt they really needed each other's support, especially with the shift to the Common Core standards. At Dewey, Jessica explained, "I think one of the reasons you have to work together is because of the way that we're delivering math. If you don't plan together it's so hard." This was particularly the case because, as we noted earlier, the school didn't use a set math curriculum:

> You can't just email everybody and say, "We're working on Chapter 10, Lesson 1." . . . We're relying on all these other sources and trying to pull things out of our book. And if one person's doing that for everybody, everybody else doesn't know what to do. Math especially, we have to plan together.

Consequently, as Victoria explained, "there's never a 20-minute meeting about math. It's always about three hours."

When collaboration feels productive, time flies and extends beyond the allotted formal time. We saw numerous instances of this across the schools. For instance, during a Billings PLC meeting, teachers were visibly engaged and optimistic about extending their collaboration in new ways that would be beneficial for them and for their students. This began when Lily said to Dave, "I wish we did designated content areas. You do social studies and I do science and then we can flip kids." The coach suggested that in her experience, this would be a great idea: "I did that with [a previous teacher partner] and it helped me become an expert in an area and also reduced planning time. I also first worked with my kids to work out the kinks, and then I took his class." The coach went on to note that in order to collaborate in this manner, "you need to really work with the other teacher on norms and expectations. For example, it helps to agree that both want a writing component or focus." She emphasized that if it works well, "it can tremendously cut down on planning time." The teachers were motivated to figure out the logistics and developed shared expectations, realizing that this would actually lighten their planning load. The entire group was animated, brainstorming ideas of shared collaboration and integrating reading, English language development, and social studies.

It is clear from these examples that teachers found relief, inspiration, and joy in the opportunity to co-plan and co-teach. This process helped them address pressing questions in their own teaching and allowed them to draw upon each other's expertise to share the workload. At the same time, the findings here also reveal how much extra time teachers are spending outside of allocated collaboration time in order to engage in this work. This can be draining on their energy, as we will discuss shortly.

Professional Collaboration as a Site for Celebrating Student Learning

Many of the teachers in this study were embedded in schools where regularly examining progress in student learning was a priority. As noted previously, this goal was pursued in a variety of different ways across the schools, but the teacher team meeting was a place where data on student progress was examined. Teachers experienced satisfaction in engaging in the examination of data together and also in celebrating successes in student learning.

Teachers commonly reflected on the need for professional collaboration in making sense of the data, particularly since this task felt unmanageable at times. At Dewey, Jessica explained:

> I think the amount of data can be overwhelming, so it's important to have a conversation with your team and figure out what's important and what's not important. Sometimes what's important to us isn't what's

important to parents. And then trying to figure out how to report it without it always looking at all the bad things that kids can't do. What are the things that they do great?

Newer teachers reflected on the fact that they did not learn how to examine data in their teacher education programs, and thus they relied heavily on the teams as a source of positive support. Kayla explained, "we weren't ever really taught and instructed on data, such as, 'This is how you read it, and this is what you do with it.'" She relied on her teammates to help her plan instructionally on the basis of the data: "I mean, we know what that means, but now what?" Like other aspects of collaboration at Chavez, the examination of data was not confined to meeting spaces. Courtney said, "Pat and I are looking at it all the time, but . . . it happens so frequently that we don't really even schedule it."

In the course of examining information on student learning, teachers experienced collective joy in students' successes. This regularly occurred in meetings at Chavez. For example, in one meeting, Courtney noted that she was "really happy with [a student's] end of the year performance . . . He really did turn around. I've seen a lot of growth." Pat "lit up" when seeing a student's performance had improved on a benchmark assessment. Teachers also shared in their students' struggles together. As Hannah noted, "You constantly want to see them growing academically. And if any kid is going backwards, that's a concern for sure . . . And it's challenging. It doesn't always work." Although these comments related to the students' performance on achievement indicators, there were many instances when teachers shared joy around students' socio-emotional growth as well.

We observed some similar patterns in teacher conversations at other schools. For example, at Anthony, a grade-level team shared in a school-wide meeting that they had seen "tremendous growth" in their students; Erica, in a very animated voice, shared that growth was not just in writing but also with students' grammar, capitalization, and the use of details. She added that they were "getting [students] to love writing" and also to "enjoy writing, sharing, and the process." This was a wonderful example of how teachers shared in students' successes together.

In teachers' conversations about student progress, there was also a clear recognition of the need to provoke joy in learning. This often came up in relation to reading. In a meeting at Billings in which student progress was examined, Lily raised the question, "What else can we do to get them to enjoy reading?" Ben recalled that they tried reading theater, and the kids loved it. He also suggested reading buddies, noting that this would not improve specific skills but would help build students' interest in reading. The principal was welcoming of these suggestions, noting that they saw the same data trends as last year in reading, and thus they needed to do things differently. Teachers were motivated to brainstorm ways to promote joy in reading. This was in contrast to the strategy of promoting better test preparation, which provoked neither teacher nor (presumably) student joy, as we will explain.

The Emotional Work of Teacher Collaboration

The Emotional Drain of Insufficient Time for Teacher Collaboration

Teachers greatly valued their time together and experienced many positive emotions as they collaborated. However, a perpetual source of stress was the insufficient time for the work. At times this was related to the administrative aspects of classroom teaching and at other times it was related to competing activities, such as mandated professional development sessions, as we explained in Chapter 5. Likewise, administrative duties had their own cycle within the school year, which interfered with time for deep learning. Kim, at Chavez, explained:

> Last week we realized, "Oh my gosh. It's been so long since we've had a good meeting, you know." . . . Because it's a staff meeting, and it's been conferences, and it's been, you know, prepping for report cards, and working with our partners on collaborating over grades. And so it's been a while since we've had a team meeting to plan curriculum.

Teachers found this administrative work to be necessary but draining, whereas meetings to plan curricula were energizing. Teachers at Dewey found themselves feeling this way, even though the activities that took away from their team time were designed to support their professional growth. As Ruby said, "We really do value that team time together to just do what we need to do to be good teachers at our grade level. I feel like a lot of that got stripped away this year, and I understand why." Teachers didn't feel the same sense of accomplishment that they would have in team time. "Nothing really stands out as, 'Oh, we really got this done.' It felt like it was all over the place," explained a teacher.

The teachers on one of the teams at Dewey felt the time required for math planning was so intense that it took away from other subjects. As Ruby explained,

> We are all basically coming in on our own time whenever we can scramble and get together. . . . There are just so many things you have to talk about as a team. So when 90 percent of it goes to math, it just, I think, leaves us feeling as though we are scratching to get more time with each other to talk things through.

In addition to finding time to collaborate for instructional planning, some teachers also wished for more time to examine data on their students—something they felt got pushed aside given the need to co-construct lessons aligned with the new standards. Jessica at Dewey remarked:

> I feel really lucky that we have a team, to see each other and work together, and we're all on the same page in terms of our expectations for our kids. We all want to use the data and not just do the test and move on with your life, but we all just want the time to do it. . . . I wish we could just sit at a table and say, "Did you guys see this?" And we could work together on it.

Jessica wished for more time to collaboratively examine data on student achievement, which there was rarely ample time for. Chavez teachers didn't face the same time squeeze because they had more dedicated time to look at data. It is clear, however, that when teachers feel that time for deep collaborative learning is insufficient, collaborative work can end up feeling draining. What might be a more sustainable model?

Interpersonal Skills for Managing One's Own and Others' Emotions During Professional Collaboration

As Day and Leitch (2001) noted, teaching requires a range of emotional repertoires in order to deal with the constant change and learning. Years ago, Andy Hargreaves (1994) described a negative teacher culture as "poisoned chalice," where teachers are antagonistic toward one another. Even when relations between teachers are not acrimonious, they may be characterized by a lack of respect or simple disregard. A significant amount of emotional work is involved in managing one's own and others' emotions within a teacher team. This effort works against the goals of professional collaboration.

The teachers at Anthony faced this challenge more so than teachers at the other schools because their culture of collaboration was not as strong. Melissa shared her experiences working with different teams and the emotions they elicited from her:

> When I was on the [previous] grade team there were some annoying key players, but you just ignore them, and the three that do get along you just deal with it, and you collaborate with each other. Sometimes you have team members that say off-the-wall stuff and they waste your time, where you're just thinking, "Oh God." They waste your collaboration time. But this year has been great because [the other grade-level teacher] and I love each other. We don't waste any time, and it's great.

Melissa went on to refer to difficult teachers as "angry birds" and described the interpersonal skills that were needed to negotiate interactions during collaboration time: "So when you're on a team with two angry birds and three that are just trying to get by and be happy, you know, you have to do this polite dance of trying to keep the peace." Clearly, interpersonal dynamics such as these can involve a great deal of emotional work on the part of teachers.

Also at Anthony, Shannon shared that one of the biggest challenges was not feeling like she had a team to collaborate with: "It's just me. The other people, other team members, kind of do what they do. So it doesn't make it easy when you [don't] have somebody you can bounce your ideas off of, which I had in the past. So that's kind of a bummer." One challenging aspect of the team dynamic at Anthony was that even when they did get along, the teachers did not have shared goals about how collaboration time would be best used. For instance, Shannon wanted more time devoted to in-depth discussions about planning lessons on writing, while Amy (who was on the same team) desired more time devoted to learning about new programs.

Although the teachers at the other three schools didn't experience complicated team dynamics, they realized that this was common in other schools. They also realized that developing positive team relationships required effort and commitment. When we visited Chavez, the school had a strong collaborative culture, but this wasn't always the case. The teachers' experience in developing this culture is instructive.

Kim reflected that years ago she found it quite difficult to work with two colleagues who had very different beliefs about teaching. She explained,

> They were very nice, but they were very worksheet oriented. They were very much, "This is the test, this is the test, this is the test, this is what we're working toward." And it was very different. Their structure of management was very different from mine. But I knew the need to collaborate, so we did a baby step.

They agreed to examine benchmark assessment results in reading and note common language arts skills across the grade level that numerous students in each class needed to work on. The teachers planned lessons to address these areas and students rotated into classrooms, based on need, one hour per week. Kim explained:

> That was our baby step, and it still gave us that common ground to discuss. And then the rest of the week everyone did what they were comfortable with. I think that was such an effective way to try and to look at your needs as a whole on the grade level.

She went on to explain that "it gave us that area that we could have the conversations about, and do some planning, and kind of add in those elements of collaboration. So that's something that helped." Kim's experience provides some insight into what might be done to bridge differences among teachers. But often, challenging team dynamics appear impossible to overcome. In those cases, what might be done?

Building relationships involves emotional work, even when teachers approach the process positively. As part of the fourth-grade team at Billings, Sheryl shared that working with a new partner was helpful, as this teacher brought different strengths to their collaboration. At the same time, the collaboration took time to build: "I think that the downside is that one thing that he and I never got an opportunity to really do is really truly collaborate. Because by the time that we figured things out, it was the end of the year."

The Emotions of Collaboration Around Data and Testing

By and large, the schools in this study had a broad focus on using evidence on student learning to inform instruction. Teacher professional collaboration thus involved examining multiple measures of student achievement in a thoughtful and reflective manner that focused on student growth. However, this wasn't always the case, and when it was more narrowly focused, it brought up feelings of frustration for teachers. The process of examining data also made some teachers feel vulnerable.

At Anthony's collaboration meetings, data were framed in terms of accountability rather than continuous improvement. This brought out negative feelings among teachers. The following vignette is from a typical meeting at Anthony:

> *In one collaboration meeting, the principal began by describing the upcoming state testing. Teachers expressed concerns to the principal about all the new testing requirements being overwhelming for the kids. Once the principal concluded the testing updates, she left to allow the team to collaborate. The team was left with 20 minutes. Luis expressed his concern that the state keeps changing things on them midstream. Instead of responding to him directly, Shannon pulled out her students' work and shared the lesson she had developed to help them for the tests. The lesson focused on using multiple online sources as evidence in their writing. She continued to share her students' work, going through the papers and pointing out what she was having them work on. The teachers discussed how they could scaffold student writing on informational essays and build stamina on the test. With 10 minutes left, the group continued to discuss how to prepare students for the math portion of the state tests. The team considered using previous grade-level tests to help students prepare. With five minutes left, Amy looked at the clock in the room and asked what time it was. Luis replied that the clock was wrong. Shannon said the correct time, which led Amy to exclaim, "Yay, we're done!" The teachers gathered their belongings and returned to their classrooms.*

This last teacher's comment reveals that the accountability focus was entirely demotivating for teachers. Teachers did not wish to spend their valuable collaboration time focused on discussing test preparation.

Even when data were examined more thoughtfully, teachers still sometimes found the process to be emotionally difficult in some ways. As a teacher at Chavez explained:

> I don't know, you feel kind of naked when your scores are laid out in front of everybody to see. And you really have to be able to answer the questions of, okay, "This student didn't meet benchmark. Why?" And you really have to be able to back up why that student met benchmark, or this student met benchmark, but they dropped three points in [the benchmark] testing. Why is that?

While she trusted her colleagues and did not feel judged by them, the process of examining data collaboratively still took some time to get used to. She added, "I was thinking, 'Oh my gosh, you guys. What happened?'" Her team had a strong culture of professional collaboration and thus she felt it was a supportive environment in which to reflect on data in relation to her teaching. Unfortunately, some teachers we spoke to in other schools did not share this sentiment.

Tight Collaborative Groups Can Become Insular

Most of this book has been devoted to discussing the benefits of professional collaboration. Indeed, we have included copious examples of tightly connected teacher teams who provide a great deal of emotional and intellectual support for each other. At the same time, tight collaborative groups of teachers risk becoming isolated from others in their school and system. While this generally wasn't a major concern at the schools in our study, these dynamics can eventually lead to groupthink and reinforce norms of contrived collegiality, rather than promoting professional collaboration for deep learning.

When teachers in our study were frustrated with shifts in their professional lives, some of them felt like retreating to their own classrooms. In a meeting with her team, one teacher said, "We say this a lot: Let's just close the door and do our own thing." A second teacher remarked, "I'm just closing the door and doing the work that we believe is strong and solid and our children are going to benefit from it." When teachers felt out of step with the district, they tended to describe the students in their own grade level as their primary concern, rather than thinking about broader issues. For example, one teacher said, "I prefer the times when we can just meet with our team and figure out what's right for our kids that are right in front of our face." She explained that her team had made its own decisions about how to interpret the new standards and what kids in their grade should know and be able to do. She recognized that there may have been some value in sharing ideas across the district, but she did not find this to be emotionally or professionally rewarding:

> These would be great conversations to have as a grade level for the entire district, I'm sure. But those meetings are time consuming, and I don't always feel that they're as on task as they need to be. Sometimes it turns more into a complaint fest than it does into productive work.

This begs the question, at what stage does this emotional safe space prevent teachers from wanting to deal with the broader school and system? A careful balance is required between nurturing a strong emotional bond between a group of teachers and ensuring that they don't become insular. When examining the emotions of teaching in relation to professional collaboration, there are complex issues to consider.

Conclusion

Leaders and teacher teams must embrace the importance of emotions in teacher professional collaboration. After all, emotions mediate people's interactions at every moment. Teachers who collaborate together often also emote together, whether in positive or negative ways. It is important to acknowledge that a range of emotions—joy, inspiration, frustration, conflict—are to be expected through professional collaboration. There are clearly more and less healthy ways of dealing with and expressing emotions in this context, however. Emotions are thus resources for action, for good or for bad. We view them as tools for action, or emotional repertoires, that shouldn't be minimized or ignored. This perspective pushes us to consider the ways in which we can both acknowledge emotions and harness them for engaging in productive professional collaboration.

Supporting teachers' socio-emotional learning should be a critical part of school change efforts. This is especially the case given that, in the current reform context, supporting the socio-emotional learning of students is becoming an important mission and vision for schools. While we have restricted our discussion to the emotions that arise in and around educational reform efforts, there are societal and political issues that affect educators' and students' emotions across international contexts (Lee & Yin, 2011; Zembylas, Charalambous, Charalambous, & Kendeou, 2011). Many teachers in the U.S. struggle daily with how to support students who experience trauma related to racism, anti-immigrant sentiments, violence, and socioeconomic realities in their communities. We cannot expect teachers to be experts in teaching socio-emotional topics in their classes and everyday schooling without practice and supports for them to enact it in their own professional collaboration spaces.

Key Takeaways and Reflection Points

- **Professional collaboration should cultivate joy in learning.** Joy can serve as a motivator for joint work; if the work is not joyful or rewarding, however, collaboration can be draining. A question for leaders and teachers alike is, how do we minimize emotional drain and cultivate joy in learning through professional collaboration? Teacher teams would be wise to assess what compels them toward joint work and what repels them away from collaboration.
- **Leaders should actively tend to the emotions that arise from collaborative work.** Professional collaboration can be bolstered with explicit strategies for acknowledging and productively managing emotions, particularly those that emerge in the context of examining results on student learning. It is important to support the capacity of teachers to embrace and develop socio-emotional learning to promote productive professional collaboration.
- **Time is a critical factor in productive professional collaboration.** Leaders would be wise to reflect on whether time constraints

associated with collaboration are contributing to teachers' emotional work. Do teachers have sufficient time for collaboration, such that it is source of joy rather than a source of stress?

References

Day, C., & Leitch, R. (2001). Teachers' and teacher educators' lives: The role of emotion. *Teaching and Teacher Education, 17*, 403–415.
Hargreaves, A. (1994). *Changing teachers, changing times: Teachers' work and culture in the postmodern age.* London: Cassell.
Lee, J. C. K., & Yin, H. B. (2011). Teachers' emotions and professional identity in curriculum reform: A Chinese perspective. *Journal of Educational Change, 12*(1), 25–46.
O'Connor, K. E. (2008). "You choose to care": Teachers, emotions, and professional identity. *Teaching and Teacher Education, 24*, 117–126.
Saunders, R. (2003). The role of teacher emotions in change: Experiences, patterns, and implications for professional development. *Journal of Educational Change, 14*, 303–333.
Schmidt, M., & Datnow, A. (2005). Teachers' sense-making about comprehensive school reform: The influence of emotions. *Teaching and Teacher Education, 21*(8), 949–965.
Zembylas, M. (2010). Teachers' emotional experiences of growing diversity and multiculturalism in schools and the prospect of an ethic of discomfort. *Teachers and Teaching: Theory into Practice, 16*(6), 703–716.
Zembylas, M., & Barker, H. B. (2007). Teachers' spaces for coping with change in the context of a reform effort. *Journal of Educational Change, 8*(3), 235–256.
Zembylas, M., Charalambous, C., Charalambous, P., & Kendeou, P. (2011). Promoting peaceful coexistence in conflict-ridden Cyprus: Teachers' difficulties and emotions towards a new policy initiative. *Teaching and Teacher Education, 27*(2), 332–341.

7

LEADING PROFESSIONAL COLLABORATION

We have shared many stories that bring professional collaboration to life, both the promise and the pitfalls. Here we review the ingredients for professional collaboration and summarize key lessons for leaders. We offer concrete suggestions for how leaders can support professional collaboration with teachers as co-developers in this complex work. Many paths can lead to improved professional collaboration. However, professional collaboration that moves toward the goal of equitable and excellent schooling needs to center on teachers' learning development, motivation, and socio-emotional needs throughout their careers.

Professional collaboration is not just about implementing promising practices or taking wholesale what has worked in other places. The context-focused approach of the four Ps work calls upon us to move beyond quick fixes that are intended to work in any context toward an approach that is sensitive to the people, practices, policies, and patterns in a setting. Every school or system has a unique set of teachers and leaders with established patterns of interaction. To move toward professional collaboration, some of these patterns may need to be questioned. Protocols for doing things, ways of talking about students, and norms of interaction can help or hinder professional collaboration, sometimes simultaneously. External policies shape the world of schools and systems more than ever before and may work in favor or against professional collaboration. While all of these things are true, we do believe that there is a set of principles for professional collaboration that can be distilled. We turn to these now.

Table 7.1 Purposeful Professional Collaboration . . .

⇒ Is driven by the goals of equity and excellence for all students
⇒ Promotes deep learning for teachers and students alike
⇒ Values broad thinking about student learning
⇒ Supports coherence but not conformity in instructional planning
⇒ Values the use of a wide range of data in informing instructional decision-making
⇒ Supports teachers in navigating through shifting policies
⇒ Embodies a genuine respect for the teaching profession and the expertise of teachers
⇒ Is a source of emotional support and develops teachers' emotional repertoires

1. Professional Collaboration Requires Mindsets Centered on Purposeful Learning for Both Students and Adults Toward Equity and Excellence

We began this book by discussing the centrality of mindsets in driving professional collaboration that is purposeful and productive. Schools, leaders, and teacher teams all have to answer for themselves given their own contexts—people, practices, policies, and patterns—the following questions: What is the purpose of professional collaboration? What goals do we want to accomplish? How do we get there? And what will it feel and look like if we are successful?

More broadly, the tasks of leaders, both formal and informal, are to make the case that collaboration bolsters student learning and achievement while also enhancing the ability of teachers to be effective professionals. Making this case requires an explicit commitment to the twin goals of equity and excellence for all students. No school leader can afford to ignore deficit beliefs about students and families. Left unchallenged, these beliefs will poison any instructional planning and data conversations that teachers engage in with one another. Beliefs and practices go hand in hand.

Beyond challenging deficit beliefs, leaders need to consider how they can support teachers and staff to focus on learning strengths for both students and themselves (Park, 2018). Just as we are moving toward more personalized and differentiated support for students, leaders need to consider how to differentiate and develop the capacity of the adults in their schools. Student learning will be reflected in the investment in teacher learning. We also need to fundamentally rethink teacher identity or change so that we discuss teachers not only as planners or implementers but also as learners, experimenters, and designers.

2. Professional Collaboration Relies on Broad Measures of Student Learning

Professional collaboration cannot thrive in a school or district where student achievement is narrowly construed. Teachers rarely engage in deep learning when gains on standardized tests are the sole measure of their students' progress or their own value added as teachers. For deep learning to occur among teachers, it must exist in a system that promotes deep learning for students. Promoting deep learning for students inevitably means thinking broadly about how to measure student achievement.

The schools we described relied on a wide range of measures to inform their understandings of student learning, and these included both summative and formative assessment measures. One of the things the teachers at Dewey also did particularly well was engage in systematic observations of their students' learning. Some teachers carried clipboards as they walked around the classroom; they documented students' learning as they worked in groups or individually, always using tools they developed themselves. District and school leaders recognized observations as one of numerous formative assessment measures that could inform instruction, and this stance communicated to the teachers that their professional judgment was valued.

3. Professional Collaboration Involves Cultivating Genuine Respect for Teachers' Professional Knowledge—Both Between Administration and Teachers and Among Teachers

A tremendous amount of expertise exists in a room full of teachers. If teachers see each other as fonts of wisdom, they are more likely to have a thirst for learning from one another. Teachers cannot work together effectively when they don't believe their colleagues bring something important to the table. In many schools, teachers make assumptions about each other's teaching expertise. Sometimes these assumptions may be based on comments teachers hear from each other—or about each other—in the staff room. Sometimes they are based on what they hear from students or parents. Rarely do teachers have the chance to observe each other and learn about their colleagues' assets and struggles first hand. This can be a starting point for building relationships, developing mutual respect, and sharing expertise. But what about teachers who do not feel comfortable sending their children to their colleagues' classrooms? These are thorny issues to address, but they must be confronted, as a team is only as strong as its weakest link.

Helping teachers see the value in each other's expertise is an important leadership role. But if the leader doesn't communicate that she or he values teachers' expertise, then teachers are unlikely to value this expertise, much less consult each other when they are struggling with an aspect of their teaching. A goal is for teachers to have high trust in their colleagues to provide a strong educational program.

4. Professional Collaboration Can Support Teachers in Valuing Their Own Expertise and Finding Ways to Support Its Development

In a professional work culture, individuals realize that they have important and unique expertise. It is important for teachers to recognize this about themselves. This is sometimes difficult in systems that have a constant churn of top-down educational reforms, signaling to teachers that the way they do their jobs is insufficient. At the same time, they need to be willing to identify the areas in which they need support from their colleagues. No one teacher is expert at everything. A willingness to admit instances where one's pedagogical or content knowledge may be weak is a critical aspect of professional growth for teachers, and these moments can turn into opportunities for professional collaboration.

Although professional collaboration is critical, it is not the only way in which teacher learning should be supported. Just as collaborative learning alone would be insufficient to support students' mastery of concepts, collaboration among teachers is insufficient for all aspects of teacher professional growth. Leaders play an important role in identifying learning opportunities for teachers that will feed their passion for the craft of teaching; leaders also buffer teachers, when possible, from professional development that is poorly planned or irrelevant.

5. Professional Collaboration Involves Garnering Coherence Around the Goals of Schooling and Beliefs About the Value of Evidence

Professional collaboration involves coherence, and coherence cannot come without some joint work. Teaching does not need to look the same across classrooms for teachers to collaborate with coherence. The teachers in this study were very different from each other and taught in ways that best fit their strengths and dispositions. Teachers at Chavez, for example, came together around common goals and assessments. But we have visited dozens of schools with common goals and assessments where teachers do not collaborate for professionalism or coherence. What makes the difference? At Chavez, teachers were working with goals and measures of student learning that they truly believed in, not those that were simply handed down from the top.

Building such a culture and structure takes time. Looking together at student work on a common task that teachers agree upon can be a useful starting point. Teachers can begin with a strengths-based conversation that includes questions such as, what does this student understand? What does this student know how to do? What's the evidence (Barraugh, 2017)? Developing common ground around these questions can spark a professional dialogue that can help to build coherence.

6. Professional Collaboration Should Include Opportunities for Teacher Empowerment and Decision-making on Key Aspects of Curriculum and Instruction

When teachers are authentically empowered, they have the ability to make critical decisions about their professional lives. Many teachers thrive with the ability to make important curricular and instructional decisions. At Dewey, where the team we profiled exemplified deep learning, teachers had the freedom to decide (within some broad guidelines) which resources would best meet students' needs. They made these decisions within the bounds of the Common Core State Standards, which they spent a great deal of time unpacking. They carefully considered exactly how and what to teach in order to ensure that their students met those standards. This process helped them operationalize the curricular standards in their classrooms, and teachers felt great ownership over the work they accomplished together. This is in marked contrast to schools like Anthony, where the curriculum was typically textbook-driven, providing teachers with much less freedom to decide how to best meet the standards.

Of course, not all teams of teachers would embrace the flexibility that the Dewey teachers had, and some might see a textbook-driven curriculum as a relief rather than an imposition. For others, however, a textbook-driven curriculum is a form of de-skilling, which can negatively impact a teacher's sense of professionalism. At the same time, teacher empowerment must be genuine rather than political and should not lead to so much work that it becomes a form of exploitation (Dillabough, 1999).

Teachers in the district where Dewey was located were provided with regular opportunities to pilot new curricular materials, programs, and other resources. A principal could offer innovations to particular groups of teachers to try if they wished. Teachers were not forced into using them but rather could experiment with them and were then asked to report back to district and school leaders about how well they worked. This promoted professional collaboration, as teachers came together to debate the merits of different writing programs, for example, and then sometimes worked together to create a hybrid approach that drew on the "best of" the programs they had tried out. To truly empower teachers is to give them some freedom over curriculum and instruction.

7. Emotions Are Resources for Action in Professional Collaboration

Professional collaboration can provide a space for social and emotional support for teachers, which is incredibly important given the various demands in teachers' professional lives. In an ideal world, all teachers would have the opportunity to participate in teams that bring them joy, inspiration, and increased expertise. For many teachers, however, collaboration is associated with feelings of being drained, stressed, or even isolated. Teachers develop emotional repertoires that involve a range of positive, negative, and even conflicting emotions within collaborative spaces. Leaders need to think about how to harness the full range of emotions for engaging in productive professional collaboration.

The intersection of professional collaboration, emotions, and time is also critical to consider. The current structure of schooling in the United States—and many other countries—doesn't provide enough time for professional collaboration, especially for deep learning. Teachers' days are already tremendously full, and it is unrealistic to imagine that the ambitious goals that policymakers, leaders, and researchers have for teacher collaboration can be realized within the space of an average school day. This is the source of a great deal of teacher stress. Ideally, the arrangement of teachers' time in the future will involve more paid time dedicated to instructional collaboration and planning. We need to find a way for systemic change since usurping more of teachers' personal time is unsustainable and will lead to burnout. While burnout is less likely if collaboration is emotionally and professionally rewarding, we cannot put the burden on teachers to find more space in their already full lives for this activity. We must give them support to develop emotional resources to deal with both the joy and challenges of professional collaboration.

8. Micropolitical Divisions Among Staff Can Thwart Professional Collaboration and Must Be Actively Addressed

We have highlighted productive and professionally rewarding forms of teacher collaboration, but we realize that many schools struggle with difficult interpersonal dynamics among teachers or micropolitical divisions among staff who have long histories. Researchers and educators alike tend to shy away from micropolitics, which are often seen as the seedy underside of organizational life (Ball, 1987). But what is a principal to do when teachers divide along gender lines (Datnow, 1998)? Or age? Or subject matter expertise, as could be the case within secondary schools (Siskin, 1994)? What is a principal to do when collaboration is hindered by the fact that teachers lack respect for a colleague on their team, sometimes for good reason? These issues are not easy to address, and they require a willingness to engage. If a teacher deems his or her colleague as incompetent, collaboration is a hard sell. Shifting the composition of teacher teams can be one solution. However, it may not always be possible given staffing constraints, and it may not be optimal for student learning. Leaders need to think carefully about how to best support both student and teacher learning alike.

9. Professional Collaboration Can Be a Lever for Continuous Improvement With an Equal Emphasis on the Professional, the Community, and the Learning That Takes Place

We noted at the beginning of the book that, in too many schools, professional collaboration rarely embodies the principles of productive PLCs. Instead, teacher collaboration often reflects another type of bureaucratic meeting mandated by district or school leadership. Devoting equal energy and time to cultivating professionalism while learning within a community is a complex endeavor. We cannot *will* productive collaboration to happen. Even when there is motivation and desire to collaborate, leaders cannot take for granted that formal spaces and times are enough. We also cannot expect that simple structures and tools will be sufficient to develop the curricular, instructional, emotional, and political competencies that teachers need to effectively engage in professional collaboration for deep learning. As such, all professional collaboration efforts must tend to the professionals who are involved and the learning that takes place among both educators and students.

Conclusion

Under the right conditions, professional collaboration can be experienced by the majority of teachers. The examples in this book make it clear that this goal is achievable. But schools will begin the journey at different places, and aligning people, policies, practices, and patterns in service of the goal of professional collaboration is an incremental but critically important process.

In sum, moving toward purposeful professional collaboration is not a reform to be implemented. Rather, it is a long-term process of rethinking teachers' professional work that requires sustained engagement on the part of leaders and teachers. Our framework equally emphasizes the notion of professional identity, the process of learning, and the sustainability of community. These elements are interdependent and must be interwoven to fully support continuous improvement that leads to equity and excellence for ALL students and for ALL teachers.

References

Ball, S. J. (1987). *The micro-politics of the school: Towards a theory of school organization*. New York, NY: Routledge.

Barraugh, A. (2017). *Student work analysis*. Presentation made at the Changing the Odds Summit, La Jolla, California.

Datnow, A. (1998). *The gender politics of educational change*. London: Falmer.

Dillabough, J. A. (1999). Gender politics and conceptions of the modern teacher: Women, identity and professionalism. *British Journal of Sociology of Education, 20*(3), 373–394.

Park, V. (2018). Leading data conversation moves: Towards data-informed leadership for equity and learning. *Educational Administration Quarterly, 54*(4), 618–647.

Siskin, L. S. (1994). *Realms of knowledge: Academic departments in secondary schools*. Bristol, PA: Falmer.

Acknowledgments

The research reported in this book was made possible in part by a grant from the Spencer Foundation. The views expressed are our own and do not necessarily reflect the views of the Spencer Foundation. We wish to thank our research collaborators, Bailey Choi and Elise St. John, for their thoughtful engagement and wisdom. We are sincerely grateful to the educators who gave generously of their time to be part of this project. We thoroughly enjoyed learning from them and deeply respect their work.

Index

accountability policies 19; *see also* Every Student Succeeds Act; No Child Left Behind Act of 2001
all students are capable mindset 22–27
Anthony Elementary School: emotions as (*see* emotions); response to shifting policies 80, 81

Bertrand, M. 23–24
Billings Elementary School 25–33; data use at 100–101; emotions at (*see* emotions); teacher meetings at 104
buffering teachers from stress of change 100–102

candid and deliberative collaboration 55–57
Chavez Elementary: common goals at 120; emotions at (*see* emotions); navigating curricular shifts collectively at 90–94; professionalism and coherence at (*see* professionalism and coherence)

coherence *see* professionalism and coherence
Collaborative Professionalism 4
collective resiliency 100–102
Common Core State Standards 69, 80, 90–94, 121
community cultural wealth 28–29
continuous improvement 73–75, 123
contrived collegiality 51–52
curriculum and pedagogy 72–73; navigating shifts in 90–94; opportunities for teacher empowerment and decision-making on key aspects of 120–121

data use in professional collaboration 5–7, 28; emotions of collaboration around 111–112
Day, C. 108–109
deep learning 60–61, 75–76; case of collaboration for 65–66; continuous improvement and innovation with 73–75; critical conversations about curriculum and pedagogy for 72–73; differentiated teacher support and

61–62; elements of, in professional collaboration 66–68; encouraging teacher teams to set their own professional learning goals and 63–65; fostering innovation and 65; sharing of ideas *versus* practices in 68–69; thinking broadly about evidence of students' 69–72
deficit beliefs 23
Dewey Elementary School: common goals at 120–121; deep learning at (*see* deep learning); emotions as (*see* emotions); reliance on broad measures of student learning 118; shifting policies and 88–90; teacher empowerment at 120–121
differentiated teacher support 61–62
DuFour, R. 4

emotions 97–98, 113–114; around data and testing 111–112; buffering teachers from the stress of change and developing collective resiliency 100–102; celebrating student learning and 105–107; emotional work of teacher collaboration and 107–113; insufficient time for collaboration and 107–108; interpersonal skills for managing 108–111; lightened feelings of "burden" 103–105; of professional collaboration, positive 100–107; and professional collaboration as source of inspiration 102–103; repertoires of 98–99; as resources for action 121–122; and tight collaborative groups becoming insular 112–113
equity-driven activity 21
Every Student Succeeds Act 22–23, 79–80

Firestone, W. A. 6
four Ps framework 9
Fullan, M. 8–9

goals: for student learning 41–44; teacher's professional learning 63–65, 120
González, R. A. 6
Grigg, J. 30

Halverson, R. 30
Hargreaves, A. 4, 8, 51, 53, 109
Hord, S. 4
Horn, I. 21

identifying student strengths as necessary to plan for student growth 27–29
innovation: continuous improvement and embracing 73–75, 123; deep learning and 65
inspiration, professional collaboration as source of 102–103
insufficient time for teacher collaboration 107–108
interpersonal skills for professional collaboration 108–111
interrupted collaboration 86–88

Jensen, B. 5

Kane, B. 21

Ladson-Billings, G. 19
leading professional collaboration 116, 123–124; addressing micropolitical divisions among staff 122–123; cultivating genuine respect for teachers' professional knowledge and 118–119; emotions as resources for action and 121–122; encouraging continuous improvement 123; including opportunities for teacher empowerment and decision-making 120–121; mindsets for purposeful learning and 117–118; reliance on broad measures of student learning and 118; supporting teachers in valuing

their own expertise and finding ways to support its development 119–120
Leitch, R. 108–109

Marsh, J. A. 23–24
measures of student learning 41–44, 118
mindsets for purposeful professional collaboration 20–35, 22, 117–118; all students are capable 22–27; identifying student strengths as necessary to plan for student growth 27–29; needs of all students-not just a narrow band- must be considered 29–32; professional collaboration as about improving both student and teacher learning 32–35

narrow bands of students, avoiding focusing on 29–32
needs of all students, consideration of 29–32
Ng, P. T. 9
No Child Left Behind Act of 2001 3, 22, 23–24, 79–80

O'Connor, M. 4, 8

policies, shifting 78–79, 94–95; Dewey Elementary and 88–90; federal, state, and local level 79–80; interrupted collaboration and 86–88; learning the nuts and bolts of 84–86; and navigating curricular shifts collectively at Chavez 90–94; opportunities to learn and 81–84
Pollock, M. 19, 29
Prichett, R. 30
professional collaboration: as about improving both student and teacher learning 32–35; across and within teams 49–51; anecdotes of 1; "buy in" for 1; candid and deliberative 55–57; change with 18–19; continuous improvement and innovation with 73–75, 123; as critical 2; cultivating respect for teachers' professional knowledge 118–119; data use in 5–7, 28; for deep learning (*see* deep learning); emotions in (*see* emotions); on the fly 51–55; framework and approach to 7–11; insufficient time for 107–108; interrupted 86–88; as key reform lever 2–5; learning the nuts and bolts of 84–86; lessening the feelings of "burden" 103–105; micropolitical divisions among staff thwarting 122–123; mindsets for purposeful collaboration 20–35, 22, 117–118; professionalism and coherence in (*see* professionalism and coherence); purposeful (*see* leading professional collaboration); relying on broad measures of student learning 118; shared responsibility in 30–31; as site for celebrating student learning 105–107; as source of inspiration 102–103; supporting teachers in valuing their own expertise and finding ways to support its development 119–120; thirst for opportunities to learn and 81–84; through shifting policies (*see* policies, shifting)
professionalism and coherence 8–9, 39–40, 57, 120; collaboration across and within teams and 49–51; collaboration on the fly and 51–55; collaborative processes for supporting student progress 45–48, 47; common goals for and measures of student learning and 41–44; support for, in collaborative spaces 48–49

professional learning communities (PLCs) 3–4; key characteristics of 5; shifting policies and 88–90

Quinn, J. 8–9

resiliency, collective 100–102
respect for teachers' professional knowledge 118–119
Ronfeldt, M. 5

scaffolded learning 27
shared responsibility in professional collaboration 30–31
Shirley, D. 9

Smarter Balanced Assessment Consortium 80
strengths, identifying student 27–29
stress of change 100–102
student learning, goals for and measures of 41–44
student progress, collaborative processes for supporting 45–48, 47

talking and reflection 8
Thomas, C. 30
time for collaboration 107–108

Wilson, B. 21

Zone of Proximal Development 27

For Product Safety Concerns and Information please contact our EU representative GPSR@taylorandfrancis.com
Taylor & Francis Verlag GmbH, Kaufingerstraße 24, 80331 München, Germany

www.ingramcontent.com/pod-product-compliance
Lightning Source LLC
Chambersburg PA
CBHW051528230426
43668CB00012B/1779